MIRACLE BE THE!

Delores Liesner's

Elk Lake
PUBLISHING™

Mission Impossible? Not with God!
Come see—God is still in the miracle business!

It is my pleasure to tell you about the miraculous signs and wonders
that the Most High God has performed for me.
(Daniel 4:2, NIV)

Dedication /Acknowledgements

Throughout scripture, we who are God's people are encouraged to dedicate ourselves, our gifts, our days, our temples, our battles, our victories, and our new things (new home, new life, new work) to our God.

…and so I dedicate this work and *your reading and application of it,* to the Lord Jesus Christ, for His glory.

My husband, Ken, and our children, Laurel (now with the Lord), Cheryl, and Kevin and their spouses have lived with the moods, whims, long hours, and endless stories of a writer. They supported, encouraged, proofread, and prayed for this project as have our grandchildren, Aimee, Michael, Ben, Kristin, David (now with the Lord), Daniel, Kimberly, and Faith.

Writer Gayle Roper told me the first thing a writer needed was a group of prayer warriors. Best friends and sisters, Marlene and Marvel, extended family, CLASS and ACFW writing clan, church family, and blog followers, Christ's presence in you has kept a light on my path through many dark and rocky travels. God placed amazing friends, encouraging editors, and grammar mavens (including Lee Warren, Kris Liesner, Deb Haggerty, and Kathi Macias), conference directors, influencers, mentors, and agent Linda Glaz and her "Glazite" team into my life.

I am so grateful for you all.

In memory of our grandson, David Penza, a portion of profits from this book will be directed to the Fullness of Life Foundation's "Give Them Wings" program, which removes financial barriers families may face by sponsoring integrative care for children with life-threatening cancer or other disease.

❧ Endorsements ❧

Be the Miracle is a book for those of us who question why we don't often see miracles in this modern day. It is a faith-strengthening reminder that God still answers prayers—sometimes in the most astonishing ways. With artful simplicity and approachable honesty, Delores Liesner recalls her real-life encounters with the God who cares about everyday things like empty freezers and gas tanks…and a child's tears.

Becky Melby, author of the *Lost Sanctuary* Series

Delores Liesner is a prayer warrior with a track record of seeing Christ work in her life and the lives of others. Her articles, devotions, and columns reflect the excitement of seeing miracles transpire, and now her book chronicles many of these amazing experiences. You'll enjoy it.

Dr. Dennis E. Hensley author, *Jesus in the 9 to 5*

Miracles are happening all around us. They scream of God's mighty hands at work on earth. We love hearing about them, we love telling others about them. But now it's time we start being a part of them. This is the challenge of faith Delores Liesner brings us in *Be the Miracle*. And you'll be up for it after reading the stories in this book.

Caleb Breakey, Author of *Called to Stay* and *Dating Like Airplanes*

My time with God in the morning is the most precious part of my day. *Be The Miracle* is a devotional filled with wonderful personal stories that will build your faith and stir your heart to receive fresh grace from God and be on the lookout for new ways to serve Him each day.

Dan Walsh, bestselling author of *The Unfinished Gift*, *Remembering Christmas* and *The Dance*

As a Christian, I sometimes forget that I serve a miracle-performing God. Delores' book not only reawakens that knowledge, but also reminds me that He still does miracles through us. Her faith in this miracle-giving God strengthens my own faith. It helps me remember that He can do the same thing through me, if I am but willing.

Gloria Penwell, assistant to the editor at AMG Publishing, assistant to the director of CLASSeminars Christian Writers Conference, and teacher and encourager at several writers conferences.

In her book *Be the Miracle*, Delores Liesner lovingly encourages and inspires us to stop observing the miracles in life from the sidelines and shift our perspective to being the miracle in someone's life. It is when we are intentionally obedient to God's mandate to give unto others that we can receive the greatest blessings of God's miraculous love and provision.

Allison Bottke, bestselling author of the Setting Boundaries series and the acclaimed God Allows U-Turns anthology

We live in a world where nearly everyone, nearly every day, needs a miracle or a touch by the Divine. *Be the Miracle* is an inspirational reminder that with God the impossible can become the possible, and we all are given the glorious honor of being a part of this holy process.

Pam Farrel, author of 40 books including *7 Simple Skills for Every Woman: Success in Keeping It All Together*

ᨪᔰᔰ Introduction ᨪᔰᔰ
Is God Still Doing Miracles Today?

Of course He is, and the stories in this little book will help you recognize some of the miracles happening all around you. Some believers are quick to discount modern miracles, but if you ask them if they've ever had a feeling that God wanted them to do something to meet a specific need in someone's life, or answered a specific prayer request, they will respond in the affirmative. I pray you will see that God wants to perform a miracle through you if you will simply obey Him.

What is a miracle?

The dictionary defines a miracle as a surprising and welcome event, not explicable by natural or scientific laws, and considered to be divine. Whether we title these unexplainable happenings miracles, God-sightings, or some other name, we love to hear of such occurrences. Why? They increase our faith by providing evidence of the miraculous in common people's everyday lives.

Are these true stories?

Yes, they are. When I've shared my stories people often say, "You must have a special relationship with God." Or "I wish things like that happened to me." I assure you we are equally special to God, and equally ordinary people who serve an extraordinary God. I'm just as surprised as anyone each time God blesses me in this manner, and there's no greater thrill for me than an opportunity to share His all-encompassing love.

Will God deliver miracles through me?

Bruce Wilkinson, author of *You Were Born for This*, says, "God is so intent on meeting people's deepest needs that He is always looking for volunteers who will become living links between Heaven and earth." When you've been unable to explain the timing or circumstances of events by natural means and the result brought glory to God, you'll understand why I and those who shared these happenings felt they were miracles.

Perhaps these stories may bring to mind similar happenings that you or someone you know has experienced. If so, I hope you'll find God's direction comforting and realize you're not alone in hearing His voice.

Get ready! God wants to stir up a desire to be a noticer, to instill the courage to be an obedient helper answering God's call, and to prepare your heart and your hands to be the miracle.

On reading these stories, you may react as I once did, realizing that sharing God's heart comes from an intimate relationship and understanding of His will. Experience this, and you'll come to know God more personally. If knowing Him more personally is your desire, read more in the final pages about the greatest miracle of all.

My goal through sharing these stories that some call miracles or God-sightings is twofold:

First, to encourage and comfort, by reminding you that the Lord won't force His will or His miracles on you. But He is looking for those who will put hands and feet to their faith—those who want to be completely His. Robert Boyd Munger, in the little book *My Heart*

Christ's Home, encourages believers to submit each area of life to Christ.

Only when we've given access—opened all the doors to every closet—does He completely fill us with Himself. That filling can be a daily or sometimes hourly process. Because I've experienced or delivered a miracle doesn't mean I no longer have difficulties. That I know God is real, present, and able to do as Philippians 4:19 indicates—to supply all my needs according to His riches in glory in Christ Jesus—is the true meaning.

Second, I pray these stories may revitalize your faith and encourage you to notice and to journal the miracles in your life so you who have been given access to all that is necessary for life and godliness (see 2 Peter 1:3) will confidently share with others that which you've received.

One final word: Please know I do not believe Jesus is a spiritual vending machine, or that God always gives us whatever we request, or that there is a magic formula for answered prayer. I do believe God cares intimately for each of us and "…the eyes of the Lord move to and fro throughout the earth that He may strongly support those whose heart is completely His" (2 Chronicles 16:9, NASB).

Remember, you are loved by the Father, lifted by the Son, and led by the Spirit!

Delores

Story Order

Resources
Last Things First
Barriers to Knowing God's Will
The Most Important Miracle

1

Surprise Us for Dinner, God!

"We're filled to capacity," the voice in the truck-stop payphone responded. "If you believe God has told you to come, then come, but I can guarantee you won't be together." Ken and I had recently accepted Christ and heard of a conference in Colorado with the Navigators, an evangelistic Christian organization. Young and naïve, we'd begun the thousand-mile trip without room reservations. We completed the fourteen-hour drive with relief—arriving awed, sleepy, and just in time to hear music signaling the first meeting.

Two hours later we were introduced to "Buzz" (Tom Buzzard), a single staff member who would share his tiny cabin with Ken, and I was directed to the sixty-four-steps-high castle turret where twenty-five single women welcomed me to a huge studio-like room with cots and clothing everywhere.

I saw Ken at breakfast and took notes beside him at evening meetings, but the workshops separated guys and gals. With so little time together all week, we had plenty to talk about on the drive home. The conference focus was spiritual growth through reading, studying, memorizing Bible verses, and praying. I was still surprised during quiet moments with God when I felt directed to give a certain amount of money to one of the missionaries. Further, I felt God was saying to give that amount of money for six months! Uncertain how to bring this up, I let Ken lead the talk on the way home. We were amazed how the separate workshops had prepared us to build up our relationship with each other and with God. I shouldn't have been surprised then, when Ken said he felt God telling him to do something that seemingly had nothing to do with the messages or workshops. When I gasped, "Me, too," he pulled the car to the shoulder and asked, "Who? How much, and for how long?" Our voices blended, stating the same name, amount, and term! Awed, Ken took my hands in his and asked God to show us how we could do what He asked because we both knew we didn't have the funds.

Once home, we tucked the children in bed, sat at the kitchen table, and spread out the budget. We'd been right. There was no extra money. Perplexed, Ken noted the only amount on the budget that equaled the commitment: food. "How can we go without food for six months?" he asked, as I wondered if God would really ask us to do something like that.

We both felt that God speaking to us separately was a miracle in itself and therefore decided we should obey. This was Thursday night. It was also payday, and Friday was our usual grocery-shopping day. I inventoried the basement pantry as Ken closed up the house for the night. He carried the few frozen packages to the kitchen refrigerator, then wiped down and unplugged the basement freezer. Carefully counting jars of home-canned fruits and vegetables and basic staples, I worried that there was only enough meat for a few meals. When we prayed beside the bed that night, the vision of the empty freezer came before me, and I conversationally told God that He'd have to "surprise us" for dinner because we weren't sure what we'd eat after those few meals.

The phone rang the next morning. Though we'd not seen or heard from my oldest brother in several years, he chose that day to call and say his wife and three boys would like to stop by for a visit and lunch the next day. I prayed my concern wouldn't show in my voice when Chris added, "Would you mind if I brought a couple of chickens for the pot for Sunday dinner?"

The first thought that shot through my mind was *Sunday? Two days of meals?* We scarcely had enough for ourselves, and now we'd have to stretch our meager provisions to feed five more people. With Chris's "see you tomorrow" still ringing in my ears, I hung up the phone and dashed to the refrigerator, where I began planning meals for the next few days.

Saturday lunch and dinner would deplete the meat supply, and we'd need something for Sunday breakfast. At least he'd offered to bring two chickens for Sunday dinner. But then what?

The next day when the doorbell rang, I raced down the stairs, happily anticipating a reunion with my brother and his family. I opened the door and saw Chris standing on the front porch.

"Oh, my goodness!" he said, slapping his forehead. "I didn't even think to ask you!"

"Ask me what?"

"If you have a freezer."

I glanced at his wife, who looked as mystified as I felt, then back at him. "Well, yes, we've got a freezer," I admitted, "but it's empty."

A big silly grin spread across Chris' face and he grabbed me in a bear hug. He then did an about-face and called to his boys to get the luggage out. He flipped up the back door on the station wagon, and under the suitcases was a blanket, which he whipped off like a magician, revealing several huge plastic coolers. His wife gaped at them, exclaiming, "No wonder there wasn't much room for luggage!" Chris laughed and told me to open the door and point the way to the freezer. The freezer! Ken, Chris, and the boys trooped past Fran and me with the coolers. Letting the door slam, we raced behind them, wondering what was going on.

Chuckling and tossing packages into the freezer, which Ken had quickly plugged in, Chris explained, "I was butchering with Fran's dad yesterday and felt this big urge to get you some meat, and to do so right away. I don't know what made me go ahead, but I'm sure glad you have a freezer."

Ken started to tell him he was an answer to prayer when I burst out laughing. I'd just noticed all the odd-shaped packages they'd tossed into the freezer were stark white! There wasn't a word on any of them. Noticing my glance, Chris looked sheepish, admitting he didn't take time to mark the packages. He offered to take them out and identify them, but Ken's eyes smiled into mine, remembering the prayer from the night before—*God, surprise us for dinner*—and we told Chris the packages were fine just the way they were.

We weren't surprised that there was exactly enough meat to last through the six monthly payments pledged from our food budget to the missionary. My faith was renewed daily as I thawed a white package to see what was for dinner, but I couldn't resist calling Ken at work on the final Thursday before payday of the six months. I'd opened the last blank odd-shaped white package from the freezer and didn't recognize the contents. The cupboards revealed little more than a partial box of macaroni and one last jar of canned tomatoes. Flipping through the pages of a picture cookbook, I identified the meat as *short ribs*. I looked through the cookbook for methods of cooking short ribs. I couldn't hold back the tears as I read, "Simmer in canned tomatoes with juice then add macaroni."

Life-Changing Lesson: God can!

The next time you have a nudging from God, take the step of obedience and watch God work. The act of sharing often takes preparation, like carrying an envelope with budgeted money for spontaneous giving, or regularly evaluating resources to see what you have to share.

This first experience of trusting God's specific guidance and provision brought us six months of daily reminders that God answers prayer. That reinforcement formed a foundation for believing that if God could orchestrate this for us, He could do anything. That same promise is yours. Remember, God only asks us to share what we have. What's in your hand to share?

Life-Changing Verse:

Make sure you don't take things for granted and go slack in working for the common good: share what you have with others. God takes particular pleasure in acts of worship—a different kind of "sacrifice"— that takes place in kitchen and workplace, and on the streets (Hebrews 13:16, The Message).

Life-Changing Challenge:

Let sharing become a habit and a lifestyle. Besides things, write down what talent, time, skill, finances, or knowledge you have that you're willing to share with others in the Lord's name, even if you never see the harvest. Ask God to show you how, where, and with whom your gift can be shared.

2

Get Out Your Wallet!

God had instructed me to give money before. We even include an amount in our budget for "spontaneous giving." But it was unusual for me to hear God's message without knowing or even seeing who was to receive the funds.

I was driving away from the Goodwill store when I felt I should return and buy for my aunt a purse I'd seen there. I pulled the car over to call my cousin and ask if her mom would like what I'd seen. She said yes, so I went in to get the purse.

I'd just stepped up to the line at the checkout when I heard the inner message, *Get out your wallet.* I obeyed, curious to see why. No sooner was the wallet resting in my hand when the next message arrived: *Take out $10.*

So there I stood in line, a $10 bill folded beside the wallet in my hand and a quirky smile on my face because I knew God was up to something. I began looking over the people in line and next to me, but I didn't feel any prompting from God that would identify the recipient. Suddenly the lady immediately in front of me kind of twitched as though she remembered something or changed her mind, then stepped out of line and headed back into the store.

Now I could see who'd been in front of her—a short Hispanic woman putting the last of a stack of children's clothing on the counter. The clerk rang her items up and took the woman's money, counted it, then apologized that she was short $10. Voila! The woman reached for the bag of clothing to see what she could put back when I handed her the money. She burst into tears. My Spanish is limited, but I knew enough to tell her the money was not from me, but from God, and that God wanted her to know He would supply all her needs.

I thought that completed the mission, but when I checked out I saw the woman and her children waiting at the exit door, looking eager yet confused. The boy, about nine, was bilingual. He asked me in English how they could ever pay me back.

I explained again that what I'd given them wasn't my money, but I was carrying the funds for the Lord, and He told me to give the $10 to them. The mother insisted she must give thanks, and her eyes grew large when I told her God would consider her thankful to spend time with Him in church the next day, which was Sunday. She looked amazed, telling me she'd been looking for a Spanish church and had asked God to help her find one. A few days prior, I'd met a Spanish pastor who used to share our church, and he'd given me their new address—just a few minutes from the Goodwill store. When I immediately responded with directions and the pastor's name, her mouth fell open and she whispered in Spanish, "God sent you with my answer."

We marveled at the timing of being in that exact spot, of God sending me back into the store, and of something nudging the woman in front of me to leave the line so I could see the one I'd been sent to bless. God was making sure we knew this was *His* plan, *His* gift, and *His* message.

I left warmed by a hug and a whispered, "Dios les bendigas" (God bless you), and the knowledge that God worked a miracle again. I love being God's delivery girl!

Life-Changing Lesson: Share what you know!

Since our first exciting experience with giving, God has supplied our needs, while also providing many unplanned and unexpected opportunities and provision to support our church and other missionaries for over forty years. I could share this message with confidence because we'd personally experienced having our needs met by a faithful God.

Only God can give specific answers to prayer for particular needs at particular times. Every truth we learn from such experiences are also meant to be shared. Share what you have, and share what you know!

Life-Changing Verse:

And my God shall supply all your needs according to His riches in glory in Christ Jesus (Philippians 4:19, NASB).

Life-Changing Challenge:

After you've written out your story of how you encountered God and how God supplied your needs, ask God whom you can encourage with your story and this verse. Pray for God's preparation of the recipient's heart.

3
The Wrong Store?

I was going to spend the day helping a friend move a recent widow from her home to an apartment. I also had a small clothing item to return to a store, so I tossed the bag in the car in case I had time between journeys across town. I prayed God would lead me to bless someone on His behalf, expecting the prayer would be answered through helping with the move. Little did I know what He was planning…

During the day, the widow understandably needed a break. Her friend offered to rest with her for an hour so I could go do my errand. As I got in the car, the thought came to me *Go to the Kenosha Kohl's*. I was on the south side of Racine so that made sense. I parked at Kohl's, automatically grabbed the bag with the item to return, and headed for the service counter. Imagine my surprise when the clerk said, "This is from Penney's. You're at the wrong store."

Hmm… I remembered that clear thought to go to the Kenosha Kohl's and knew I must be there for a reason. Then I saw a woman looking longingly at a dress. Now don't think I'm crazy—I knew I was there for her, but not why. I went up and asked if I could help her. She asked if I worked at the store, and I said no. She said, "Well, that's okay because I was just…um…thinking… You know, feeling sad how I can't wear a dress like this anymore because of some scar tissue I have by my tummy. I've looked for answers everywhere and asked several medical people, but no one seems to know if there's anything that can be done."

I'd just been to a new doctor the week prior and learned of a few things that could alleviate identical symptoms, so I said something like, "Well, isn't the Lord good! I just learned that last week. Here's what you can do about—"

"The Lord?" she interrupted.

For a second I thought I'd be in trouble for talking about the Lord, but then she spoke again, thoughtfully. "So you're a Christian…" She opened her purse to show me something, shyly admitting she wasn't just *thinking* about the dress; she was also praying as she looked at it. "I asked God if He could send me someone with an answer. Then I thought what a silly little thing that was to ask God, but…" She paused reflectively. "But here you are." Her voice had drifted into a whisper as she pulled out a Bible study book and showed me what she'd been studying.

While we marveled at God's caring about every detail in our lives, I happily wrote the information and the doctor's name inside her study book as she'd requested—for *proof* that God had really led me there for her.

There we were, two strangers in the junior department at the Kenosha Kohl's, hugging, and thanking God for bringing us together.

As I headed to my car, I realized several things. One was that God used my hyperactive personality to not look at the shopping bag in the car. If I had, I would have seen it was for another store, and I wouldn't have gone in. Another was that God had trained me for this moment to recognize His direction from my own self-talk. And finally, I couldn't help a smile creeping across my face when the thought dawned on me…

Guess I wasn't in the wrong store after all.

Life-Changing Lesson: Live expectantly!

That young woman believed in prayer, yet when she prayed she was surprised, not so much that God had answered, but at *how* He answered. When I hear God telling me to go somewhere or speak to someone, I expect something to happen. Why? Because I've had the experience before. Micah, in the verse below, could confidently state "My God *will*…" because he too had experienced God's miraculous working in his life. We also have cause to trust, to hope, and sometimes to wait patiently because God will fulfill His promises.

Life-Changing Verse:

But as for me, I will watch expectantly for the LORD; I will wait for the God of my salvation. My God will hear me (Micah 7:7, NASB).

Life-Changing Challenge:

What are you expectantly watching God to do? After you've written out how God has already answered prayers for you, ask Him for an opportunity to bless someone with this hope, and expect Him to answer!

4
A Heavenly Recipe

"Okay, Lord, you've got my attention" didn't sound like much of a prayer, even to me, after the miracle of getting a home when we'd been so in debt. But I knew God understood.

When we'd moved in the day before, I'd promised I was going to live on what we had. No more charging things and then challenging God to provide the payment a month later. He apparently intended to take me at my word—and He was acting through Laurie, our first-grader.

Out of breath and distraught, our little girl had been a block away from home, heading for school, when she realized she'd forgotten to tell me she was supposed to bring cupcakes for the class—TODAY! She turned around and raced back with the news.

With two days until payday and not even any spare change in the house, I'd answered her pleading brown eyes with an extra kiss and a promise to be there at noon with the cupcakes. She bounded down the stairs again, happy, and I giddily called after her, "Don't worry—no problem!"

But there *was* a problem. Two minutes later, imagining Laurie's trusting smile when I delivered on the promise, I rummaged in the unpacked boxes for baking tins and the mixer. I confidently set them on the counter then opened the refrigerator, only to discover there were no eggs. No eggs? How could I make cupcakes without eggs?

"Now what?" was my next prayer. But I'd no sooner prayed than I became frantic as I tried to figure out how *I* could fix the problem. The little voice inside whispered, *Haven't you learned ANYTHING? That's how you got into trouble before. Trust Me. Pray!*

Pray? For eggs? I looked at the clock—already past nine. I was running out of time, and I was mystified—mystified because the most unusual peace had replaced my "normal" frantic feeling over the possibility of breaking a promise. One word had brought that peace: Pray. The word hung before me, enticing and sweet as the smell of fresh laundry on the clothesline.

I surrendered. *"Okay. I promised to take You at Your word, Lord, and You've surely shown me by getting us into this home what You can do with little things like eggs. Please help me keep my word to my little girl, and keep my promise to You not to spend what I don't have."*

The next step was an act of faith. I turned on the oven and measured all the ingredients as our preschooler lined the tins with paper cups. We'd just finished making—and sampling—the frosting when I heard the mailman close the box on the front porch. Of course! God could send us a refund check or something in the mail. I rushed to the porch and almost, as they say, "swallowed my teeth"—for there, neatly stacked under the mailbox, were two blue dozen-sized cartons of eggs.

Surely mailmen didn't bring eggs! I laughed, as our little preschooler joined me on the porch chanting, "Eggs! Eggs!" We ran to look out over each side of the big open porch that lined the front of our house, glancing up and down the street. No mailman; as a matter of fact, no one was in sight.

Leaving the mystery for the moment, we raced in the house and got those cupcakes finished, cooled, frosted, and delivered shortly before noon.

"They look homemade," the teacher said as she greeted me at the door.

"Yes, it's…um, a heavenly recipe." I smiled, thinking of the morning surprise. Laurie waved and grinned her thanks as the teacher closed the door, and Cheri and I walked back home wondering about the mysterious eggs.

The luxury of two-dozen eggs appearing on the porch and the baking utensils still on the counter convinced me to treat my husband later that evening. Gingerbread, a favorite dessert of ours, came to mind. As I was measuring the ingredients, the thought came to make a double batch so some could go in lunches the following day.

Later that day, I grabbed the ringing phone just as Cheri ran and threw her arms around Ken's legs when he came in the front door. My mind only partially registered his words when he asked, "What smells so good?" because my garrulous friend Bonnie's voice was asking at the same time, "Did you find some eggs on your porch?"

"Was that you?" I exclaimed. "I looked and didn't see anyone. Why would you leave eggs on my porch?"

"Well," she said, in her typical one-breath paragraph, "about eight or so this morning I got the strongest urge for gingerbread…" I glanced, surprised, at the still steaming pans on the stovetop. "…and, well, you know I can't bake, but I thought of you and how much I like gingerbread. I know things are tight for you just getting into your house, and I thought maybe if I bought the most expensive ingredient, you'd make me a batch…"

"Gingerbread?" I croaked, as she continued.

"David offered to go to the store before school to get the eggs," she explained, "and he was supposed to ring your bell and give them to you. But he just now got home from school and informed me he left them on your porch but forgot to ring the bell. That's when I decided to call to be sure you found them."

I sucked in my breath as she finished her tale. "Desperate, huh? So would you consider making—"

"Gingerbread?" I said, interrupting her mid-sentence. "No problem."

I laughed, playfully wagging my finger no to Ken's attempts to sneak a taste before supper. "But first, let me tell you about our morning."

Amazed laughter and joy soon filled two kitchens as the story of the cupcake prayer unfolded. To this day the smell of gingerbread is a reminder of a heavenly recipe: For a lesson in trust—just add eggs!

Life-Changing Lesson: Trust!

Worry often follows commitment. Will I be able to fulfill my promise? Should I have been so public in my declaration? Will this cause embarrassment to the cause of Christ if I fail? If I depended on my own abilities, I'd let those worries consume me, but if I depend on God's abilities and know the commitment I'm making is in His will, then I can't lose.

Life-Changing Verse:

For I am the LORD your God, who upholds your right hand, Who says to you, "Do not fear, I will help you" (Isaiah 41:13, NASB).

Life-Changing Challenge:

Trusting someone who shows they care deeply for you is easy. God reminds us that He is our God—the One who breathed life into us and the One who upholds, supports, refreshes, and strengthens us, and who loves us at great cost. God is the one who gives us vitality, the capacity to live, grow, develop—the power to survive. This is the One Who says to us, "Do not fear, I will help you."

If you've answered His offer to be *your* God, whether in this moment or long ago, write out three things you'll trust Him for. Then read this verse daily for a week to rout the enemy as you are reminded that the great I AM is the One Who will help you.

5

Love Letters from God

I met our pastor's cantankerous grandmother only once—when caroling at her home with our youth group the previous Christmas. As soon as we finished singing, Grandma Edith calmly stated, "Okay, you can go now." She'd been irascible and rude to family and stranger alike. Edith was markedly uninterested in spiritual things, and though our prayer group prayed for her often, I'd never intentionally thought to visit her—or unintentionally, for that matter.

On our way to visit an old friend at the hospital, my husband led the way to the elevator. Running through my mind was the verse I'd read that morning in 1 Corinthians, about becoming "all things to all men." It had been years since we'd seen the man we were coming to visit. As the door closed, I softly prayed, "Lord, show me who or what I should be for our old friend." I had no idea what God was going to do.

My whisper had no sooner ended than the elevator dinged, and the door slid open to reveal Pastor John, his wife, and one of their sons. They told us Grandma Edith was in the hospital again, and they'd taken a break from her obviously dementia-related angry outbursts to visit a friend on another floor. We offered to stop by her room and say hello if our visit didn't last too long with our friend. They warned us she was in unusually bad form—testy and ornery, making unkind remarks to everyone in the room.

Surprisingly, no one was in our friend's room. The nurse informed us he'd been released more quickly than anticipated and had gone home just a short time before our arrival.

We shrugged and decided we must be there to visit Grandma Edith. On the way back to the elevator, Ken said a quick prayer for family members to find peace in the midst of the situation. In the surprise change of direction, I'd forgotten about the verse I'd read in 1 Corinthians until the next scene unfolded like a mystery drama.

We could hear Edith as we approached, rudely admonishing her grandsons. But when I entered her room, she turned toward the door and paused, her eyes large and her mouth making a round *O*. She looked me in the eye, opened her arms to me, and cried out, "You came! You came!"

Our pastor's son faced me from a chair on the opposite side of the bed, and Pastor, his brother, and their wives all stood along the wall at the end of the bed. We looked at one another then back at Edith. I even looked behind me in case I'd misunderstood her greeting. But Edith quickly called to me, ordering me to have a good visit and make up for all the time lost since we'd last seen each other. I hedged, telling her I hadn't thought she'd remember me at all.

"Remember you!" she all but shouted. "Of course I remember you! We worked together fifty years ago!" Pastor's son doubled over in laughter at the look on my face, both hands shielding the sound but unable to hide his body's shaking.

I tried again, not wanting to upset Edith. "I don't think I'm who you believe I am, Edith."

"Of course you are," she insisted, telling me she had a picture somewhere of the two of us having lunch together at a picnic table outside of work. In vain, I continued trying to convince her of who I really was, but she'd have none of it. Finally I closed my eyes a second, asking, *Lord?*

The silent answer came in the words of the Scripture I'd read earlier that day: *Be all things to all men.* I turned and looked toward Pastor and shrugged, signaling that if Edith so desperately wanted me to be someone special in her life, I was going to accommodate her.

He nodded back his approval, and I said, "Edith, as long as you're so glad to see me, how about if I share what God's been doing in my life these past years?"

She was eager to hear anything I had to say at that point, letting me share my testimony, miracles God had done, and how I discovered the Bible was written for us. She snapped back, "Maybe for you, but God wouldn't want to talk to someone as ornery as me."

I asked her if she got love letters from someone who truly cared about her, wouldn't she put them in a special place and take them out and read them every day? She agreed, and when I told her that's what the Bible was—God's love letters to her—she sighed wistfully.

I knew others in the room were praying, and I heard their intake of breath when Edith said, "I never thought about the Bible that way before." She allowed me to pray for her, and when I asked her to pray, she brought us all to laughter with her honesty when she said, "God, thank you that Delores came and talked about these things, but you know I'll probably go right back to the way I was."

Edith was sent to a nursing home for rehab the next day. When Pastor John's wife entered the room to visit, Edith shocked her again, demanding she go back home and bring that large-print Bible her grandson had talked about because she wanted to read those love letters from God.

A few days later, I intentionally visited Edith, hesitant and curious if she'd remember the hospital incident. Her greeting of "Where have you been?" answered my question. I was still her mystery friend.

"Sit down and read," she ordered, pointing to her book of letters from God. I felt awkward at first, posing as her long-remembered co-worker and acting without a character description. Then I recognized her hope or expectation of a friend was really the same as all of us: someone who loves us just as we are and has the time to hear about our pain.

Several months later, prayers for family peace had been answered, knowing their grandma had a personal relationship with the Author of those love letters. They had assurance that she knew she'd soon be with Him.

I still chuckle at God's sense of humor because Edith never did believe what she called my *teasing* of who I was...or wasn't. I hope someday I'll get to meet the person Edith saw when I walked in the room. I'd love to thank her for being the kind of friend so long ago that would eventually inspire Edith to welcome God's message so warmly. I have a feeling Edith's other friend also knows the Author of those love letters, and now knows how God turned an act into a friendship.

Loved by the Father. God knew before the beginning of this story that Edith's heart would cry out to Him for a friend. He knew I'd be in that hospital and have that verse on my mind that day. How loving for Him to give me the idea of love letters from God—to cause Edith to see what no one else could see, to allow me to see Him within a crabby, hardened, little old lady, someone who longed to know love. Love begets love, and we all were amazed at God's miracle performance. I truly did have to act at the beginning because Edith had a caustic tongue. But repeatedly practicing God's presence in an almost surreal situation tweaked each performance into the reality of caring.

Life-Changing Lesson:

Be ready to try to see things from another's point of view.

Life-Changing Verse:

To the weak I became weak, that I might win the weak; I have become all things to all men, so that I may by all means save some (1 Corinthians 9:22, NASB).

Life-Changing Challenge:

Are you willing to disembark (get out of your boat, your place of safety) and let God reveal whatever He needs to show a seeker? Only with God's help can we come to be that which the seeker needs to see and hear.

Write out your spiritual story, remembering what you needed to see and/or hear to come to God, and note who played those roles in your life. Then watch and listen for those needs from others.

Are you willing to become what God needs you to be in order to present Him to those who are seeking Him?

6

Phone Home

Barb peeked around the office door she held open, thinking I was right behind her. "Forget something?" my co-worker asked, as I stood there looking perplexed.

An urgent prodding—*Call Ken now; he needs you*—rang through my mind. I stopped in my tracks, momentarily startled. Thinking of all the errands I had to do, I hesitated, wondering at the reality of the unexpected mental command.

"What's wrong?" my now concerned friend asked, approaching me.

"I have to call home. Ken needs me," I replied, turning back into the office.

She followed, quizzing me as we walked around the counter heading for the nearest desk phone. "What just happened here?" she asked, looking at me oddly. "Didn't you have a list of errands to do? I didn't hear the phone ring. How do you know he needs you?"

"I just know it's urgent," I said and requested she wait as I dialed our number.

The sense of alarm grew as Ken's voice came weakly over the receiver.

"Honey, what's wrong?" I asked.

"I don't know," he mumbled. "Sick. Headache. Can't remember if I took aspirin."

My strong hero who never seemed to get ill sounded so far away! "Do you want me to come straight home?" I asked, for I was already mentally canceling my errands while trying to calm a mounting fear.

"Yes. I need you." He unknowingly echoed my inner message, and I quickly assured him I'd be right there.

Barb's eyes widened as I told her something was wrong with Ken then raced out of the office. "Call you later," her voice echoed, as I let the outer door slam behind me.

My daughter lives next door and happened to be on the porch in time to see and hear my car come to a screeching halt. She called out in alarm, and I yelled for her to get her husband, Frank, not knowing if I'd need help.

I found Ken on our bed, curled into a fetal position, mumbling about meatloaf and aspirin. I immediately dialed the triage of our medical clinic, thanking God when I was connected with a nurse-friend who calmly instructed me to get Ken to the emergency room. She assured me she'd set up his initial admittance.

Frank helped me get Ken into the car and to the hospital. By the time we arrived, I knew something was really wrong as he couldn't tell the nurse where he was. A medical team soon surrounded him. I backed out of the way as they came with syringes, tubes, and a monitor. Some time later they took Ken for tests while I went back to admittance to complete signing papers and answering questions. I explained his condition when I found him and that he'd been fine when I left the house that morning. I also told them how I was just leaving the office to do errands that would have taken an hour or two when I heard or "felt" the urgent message: *Call Ken now; he needs you*!

Finally the doctor in charge called me from behind an emergency room curtain. He explained that Ken appeared to have had a stroke and that he'd been brought in just in time to receive medication to stop the attack. He questioned me thoroughly as to his health and activities in the past several days. Two other doctors joined him, both insisting Ken must have been ill and called me for help, or that he was ill that morning and I called to check on him before leaving work, or that we always called each other at that time of day. Feeling as though I were being grilled on some police show, I finally realized the admittance nurse must have repeated my story and how incredulous my tale must have sounded.

Each time one of the doctors made a new suggestion of what *really* happened, I repeated the story again for all the onlookers, until one doctor summarized his feelings by skeptically raising his eyebrows and asking if I was saying that God told me to phone home. I couldn't stop the smile that spread across my face as my heart and voice affirmed, "Yes. That's *exactly* what happened." He walked away, shaking his head in disbelief, only to return with a neurosurgeon who also wanted to examine Ken and hear the story again.

Ken had returned to normal by that time and was amazed to hear about what stirred me to call him. We were shaken as the doctor explained that if I'd done my errands before I returned home, the medication to help Ken would have been too late. Sobered at the narrow escape, Ken quietly agreed to follow the doctor's recommendation of an overnight stay for observation. Word apparently spread, as the following day was filled with a parade of nurses, doctors, and lab technicians checking on him, shaking their heads in wonder and asking, "Are you the one?"

For several months after, cautionary repeated testing still showed absolutely no damage or evident result of a stroke, and I was asked to join Ken for an exit appointment. The goal, the nurse explained, was to see if the patient had omitted sharing any changes or side effects of the trauma—if he indeed had returned to normal. The doctor chuckled when I assured him my husband was as "normal" as I'd ever seen him. He laughed outright at Ken's teasing thankfulness that for once his somewhat rebellious wife had listened to a "still small voice" of authority.

We all joked a bit, but the lowered tone of the doctor's voice as he left stopped our teasing. Like the conversation bubble in a cartoon, the words seemed to hang in the air as he confirmed there was no other explanation for Ken's continued health than the perfect timing of a "message" to phone home. Awestruck, we gazed at each other, repeating the doctor's whispered conclusion as he left the room: "Amazing."

Life-Changing Lesson: Hearing anticipates action!

Do you know the Master's voice? Knowing or recognizing the Master's voice comes after time spent together, as does hearing or understanding His messages. Sometimes I've failed to obey immediately and regretted my delay. I was so humbled to recognize the different way this story could have ended had I not heard the voice and recognized the urgency to obey.

Life-Changing Verse:

*My sheep **hear My voice**, and I know them, and they follow Me...* (John 10:27, NASB, emphasis added).

Life-Changing Challenge:

In 1 Samuel 3:10b, when the boy Samuel finally understood that the Lord Himself was speaking to him, he declared "Speak, for Your servant is listening." Are you like that—pencil ready, eager to truly hear and understand God's message with intention to follow whatever He commands? Just as you know what your spouse or boss would do in a given situation, spending personal time with God will help you know the Master's voice, expect to hear His voice, and be ready to obey. As you complete your daily reading, write out what God is directing you to do, then watch for the opportunity to fulfill His desire for you.

7

Sowing Seeds in Indiana

My daughter-in-law, Kris, was puzzled. "What was that about?" she asked.

Once again, the timing amazed me. We were on the way home from a two-day natural health workshop, after being sidetracked from our original plans. One of the women at the workshop wanted to go to a nearby park to relax and trade notes. That sounded like a good idea, as all of us were sleepy after the full morning of lectures.

Finally on the road, I'd just commented that at least we'd missed the Sunday noon rush at area eateries when Kris spotted a little family restaurant and directed me into the parking lot.

Seated in a booth, Kris faced me, her back to the middle-aged couple I watched across the room. The man, a balding Hispanic, reached across the table to grasp the hand of his softly-rounded and slightly-graying wife. Together they bowed heads in prayer over a simple meal of soup and a shared sandwich.

When we got our bill, I asked the waiter about the couple. He said they came there every Sunday. When I whispered to him that I wanted him to add their tab to ours but not to tell them until Kris and I left, he hurried off, leaving me to wonder if he didn't hear me. But Kris had noticed the waiter's bright eyes and eager expression, and she was curious to see what he'd do.

My daddy taught me to be a noticer, and when possible, to follow God's leading and cover the cost of a meal for strangers. The trick was to give the waiter a note (a Bible verse or whatever message God led me to write for the recipients) and leave before the note was delivered.

Instead of the waiter, a skeptical manager approached our table, wondering if I was playing a prank. I assured him I wasn't and gave him my credit card. As he turned toward the register to process the charge, we saw the waiter heading directly to the couple, my little pass-it-on card in hand. I'd hoped to be gone before this happened, but we were still waiting for the manager's return with my card and receipt. I could see the man read my note, pass it to his wife, then rise from the booth and head for us. Kris later told me she could also see the waiter hovering behind our booth, watching.

The gentleman explained he was a pastor of a fledgling Spanish church with declining attendance. That day had been the lowest turnout yet. Saddened, he questioned God if he should give up the church. He and his wife had just asked God for a sign of encouragement when the waiter brought the note, which read, "God will bring the increase."

The profuse thanks was embarrassing, and Kris joked later that I'd made two grown men cry. But at the time, I could only point the waiter and the pastor to the One who'd known the time and the place, and arranged both meeting and message. The wife then asked if they could pray for me.

Now I must admit I was skeptical (shame on me!) as the wife prayed that the financial blessing would soon return to me, multiplied a hundredfold. But despite my doubt, the blessing that started there in Indiana came a few days after returning home. The blessing came in the form of a surprise call from an area home-improvement place where, over a year ago, we'd complained about a defective product that cost $1200. When local management would do nothing to remedy the situation, we contacted the district offices and were basically told "too bad," that incidents like ours were why they had *almost* 100% satisfaction." We were stunned, to say the least. After months of calls and no results, we concluded we'd had another expensive life lesson, replaced the item from another vendor, and stowed the defective one in the basement.

Now a surprised and humbled manager said one of my messages from a year ago somehow turned up on the desk of the right person at corporate, and the manager had been told to call me that day to apologize and tell me they had $1200 in cash for me to pick up. The Indiana prayer was answered—specifically and in God's timing. We were able to meet a need that arose that morning and to save a portion to bless others again.

I wish I'd asked for the pastor's address so I could tell them that I, too, had received a great reminder that in His time, God will plant a seed and increase the harvest to provide our needs.

Life-Changing Lesson: Giving is an act of preparation and worship.

Have you been able to look back and recognize God preparing your heart for an act of kindness? Did you realize you were worshipping God by letting His will root and grow in you so you could be the blessing others need?

Life-Changing Verse:

Now He who supplies seed to the sower and bread for food will supply and multiply your seed for sowing and increase the harvest of your righteousness (2 Corinthians 9:10, NASB).

Life-Changing Challenge:

Plant a seed of faith. Pay it forward…and watch God multiply your own harvest. Prepare your seed, perhaps $2.00 and a message in an envelope. Place whatever amount God directs in your wallet or purse, and ask God for guidance to deliver the money in His name and for His glory. Praying before sharing is as important as preparing the soil in your garden for seeds. Praying after the sowing leaves the yield to God's cultivation and the result to His glory.

Ready? Then take that step of faith and deliver your seed!

~✣8✣~
The Translation Triangle

Sometimes dreams come true in the most unexpected ways.

Break time in our busy elementary school was a haven from stress. In this oasis we'd share a laugh to lighten the day, and sometimes let slip a dream or two—where we'd like to go, what we'd like to do, things we knew would likely never happen. And then one did.

Our school district offered a brief course consisting of phonetically pronouncing and memorizing sentences to enable us to guide Spanish speakers enrolling their child in kindergarten. I was excited to take the class, even if it meant I only learned a dozen or so simple sentences: *Please write your name here. What is the child's age and birthday? What is your address?* God had given me a love for the Spanish-speaking people, and consequently one of my recurring dreams was to visit missionary friends in Mexico.

An older member of the staff, about to retire, laughed with me about someday going to Mexico or Spain and only being able to say things like, "Write your name here." One day after lots of laughter, Dianne met with me privately and reminded me of a story we both loved. It was about a little adopted girl, who'd never had a birthday party, so she misunderstood the purpose of birthday money when she received it. Instead of buying things for herself, she used the money to buy gifts for her new family and friends. Dianne mentioned how that story inspired her, and rather than have a retirement party with gifts she really didn't need, she wanted to pay for my airfare to visit my friends in Mexico...*if* she could come along. Of course I agreed. She insisted the glorious gift was as much for herself as for me because she wanted to be there and see my dream come true.

There was no time to take an official class to learn Spanish, nor would I need to be fluent, as the missionaries would translate for us. Often, as I leave on trips, God gives me a particular thought or verse for each adventure or mission. I sometimes prayed the words of songs and was very touched by one called "Be Not Afraid." One line says, "You shall speak your words in foreign lands and all will understand."[1]

That became my prayer for the journey, that I could somehow communicate with a Spanish-speaking person and we would understand each other.

As recent language-school graduates, the missionary couple was painstakingly exact with their speaking and translation. They shared humorous examples of a recent visitor who'd said "hello" in Spanish. Receiving eager, high-speed responses, he thought he'd be safe to keep answering "yes." Of course, he had no idea what he was agreeing to, so the Spanish-speaking group had a little fun, knowing "yes" was the limit of his language skill. I laughed with them, but for once decided I'd keep quiet and listen.

Each day we travelled with the missionaries, visiting various pastors and their communities. Each pastor welcomed us and took us to their home or church and shared their stories in Spanish, which our missionary friends then translated into English for Dianne and me. The Mexican people were so welcoming and unassuming that we were very comfortable with the situation until the final visit.

When we arrived for that last visit, the missionaries, as usual, greeted the pastor and asked him to share his story. By now, though we didn't actually understand, we recognized the greeting and gestures as the same greeting given previous pastors. Then the pastor directed comments to the missionaries, but the blank looks on our friends' faces let us know this visit was not going as usual. They surprised us by apologizing and explaining they couldn't understand the pastor. I was mystified after watching the pastor nod his head in response to their introductory words, so I knew the pastor understood Phil and Norita.

Imagine everyone's surprise when, after listening to the confession, I blurted out to the missionary in English, "But how can you not understand the pastor? I understood what he said."

All eyes zeroed in on me, as one of the missionaries who served as a translator blinked in obvious confusion. "You did?"

I nodded my head in affirmation.

"How could you?" the missionary asked.

"I don't know, but I do."

After a moment of stunned silence, Phil asked what I thought the pastor said. I explained in English, and he translated my words into Spanish for the pastor, who agreed it was indeed a direct quote. From the expression on the pastor's face, we could tell Phil first explained to the pastor that he couldn't understand him, but I, who spoke only English, said I did.

All of our eyes widened in surprise as Phil translated that the pastor declared God was doing something very profound. He had badly wanted to explain what God had done and to share their prayer requests, and now the five of us—two bilingual English/Spanish, two English and one Spanish dialect—could understand one another.

An unprecedented triangle of translation enabled the hour of visiting to continue. The pastor, now facing me, would speak; I would then share in English what he'd said, along with my own comment; then the missionaries replied in their Spanish dialect, and around the conversation went.

When the pastor closed our visit in prayer, he thanked God for the profound experience of a three-cornered conversation in a foreign land. When he said "foreign land," the words of the song came to mind and tears filled my eyes. What a holy and amazing experience!

We drove off discussing which message God wanted us to hear. Was it the pastor's words, the lesson that language is no barrier to God, or the sad fact that if it hadn't happened to us, we likely wouldn't have believed the story?

Life-Changing Lesson: Expect surprises from God.

In Acts 2, when the Day of Pentecost came, "they were all in one place." They were expecting something to happen, anticipating the God of all authority to work. Greeks were there, Romans, Nazarenes, and Jews. They apparently didn't anticipate that each one present would understand in their native languages what those of different languages were speaking. God always seems to do more than we expect, but we should expect surprises!

Life-Changing Verse:

*And how is it that we each hear them in our own **language** to which we were born? (Acts 2:8, NASB, emphasis added)*

Life-Changing Challenge:

That pastor was explaining his testimony and teaching with Scriptures. God has similarly placed pastors and teachers in our lives to explain the Scriptures. Many say the Bible is too hard to understand, but the only barriers to understanding the Scriptures are unbelief and apathy. Challenge yourself to take one verse a day to ponder and read with great eagerness, then ask God to amplify the meaning in your life, just as the new believers did in Acts 17:11. (See How to do a Verse Study at the back of this book.)

9
Gift of Grace

When the court called to ask if I'd be guardian for my mother, I wanted to shout, "NO!"—but I knew there was no one else. Mother's illness had caused her to change into a difficult personality, which alienated most family members as well as many from her community. After a lifetime of abuse, I had no relationship with my mother to build on, but I knew the Scriptures said to honor your parents. I was duty-bound. Stuck. Trapped. So I sighed and whimpered yes, I'd be her guardian. Obedient but reluctant and fearful, I did as instructed to renew contact.

Prior attempts to survey Mom's health and living conditions were met with anger, weapons, and hurtful words. I won't deny the emotional storm that rode into town with me (and my accompanying granddaughter) when I answered the call of the court for a guardianship hearing. That day God instructed me to love Mom without words, and my animated eighteen-year-old granddaughter, Aimee, made my silence possible. Her chatting allowed me to concentrate while driving Mom to see her sister, the family farm, and the homes and schools where she'd experienced good memories. Mom loved eating and enjoyed being served at Four Seasons, a fancy resort built on Miscuano Island. Knowing she'd want several things on the menu, we prearranged for the waitress to wrap several choices she wanted but didn't order.

The end of that day was really a new beginning. Before I left, Mom asked me to help her remove her shoes. I knelt before her, and she touched my head like a benediction, surprised that her little girl had silver in her hair.

Seeing God honor Mom through my silence that day confirmed she needed nothing from me but to be a carrier of God's grace, to share the extravagant love I'd experienced. Suddenly the solution seemed so obvious: how could I give any less than I'd been given?

Finally freed from the insidious trappings of guilt, bitterness, and responsibility, I changed from *taking care* of her (act of blind obedience, *have* to do it) to *giving care* (act of choice, *blessed* to do it). With that realization, new life was breathed into our relationship.

When I read the original meaning of grace (from Ephesians 1:6 *charis:* to *grace*, i.e., *endue* with special *honor—make* accepted), I had a new incentive. An idea and an urgency rose up to plan Mom's coming birthday as a way to honor her. Mom often mentioned she wished she'd written a book of her life story. Never Too Late was the appropriate name of a senior "wish program" that enabled the raising up of Mom's memories for a special gift. The group helped secure a young English teacher from a nearby college to interview Mom and record stories from her life in her own words. Months later Erin e-mailed me the narratives to combine with old photos and recipes. The result was a giant-sized memory book in her favorite pastel pink, which was completed in time for her big day. When I read the story about how Mom had entertained seniors years ago in the very place that was now her home, I recalled some letters stuffed in a scrapbook. Sure enough, one detailed her pride in participating in the Senior Follies and included the name of the fellow who began the events. I was able to locate him through the Internet, and he provided a video of Mom singing and tap-dancing for the "old folks" when she was in her seventies. Our son helped transfer that onto DVDs—one of the entire program and one containing only Mom's solo, which she could watch anytime she needed a reminder that she really had performed.

Knowing Mom was proud to be politically involved, we contacted current and past presidents and her state's governor for birthday wishes. All seven sent cards or autographed photos that she displayed and bragged about to anyone who'd listen.

On her birthday, she proudly wore purple with a matching corsage and sat among family and friends, as well as the staff and residents of her homecare center. Each person who greeted her added a flower to the growing bouquet. Her face lit up, eyes aglow at the giant pink memory book, proudly confirming the stories as they were read back to her. At ninety-three, she'd already forgotten sharing them and wondered how the reader knew she'd learned to bake at nine years old and carried lunch to school in Karo syrup pails. Tears of happiness came when everyone applauded while watching her Follies' singing and dancing. "See?" she said. "I did something good for others."

Hours later, after the last guest wished her a "Happy Birthday," I brought her to her room for lunch. "I don't think I can eat a bite," she said. "I'm already filled up—filled up to the top with happiness."

"Me, too, Mom," I croaked, surprised with the joy of the moment.

I hadn't known until then that you can't give the gift of grace without receiving that gift right back.

Life-Changing Lesson: *Do* Grace.

God allows difficult people in our lives so we'll appreciate the grace

He's already shown us and to teach us how to grace others. Grace is sharing God's love with others in the same exuberant and generous manner in which God gave grace to us. God's grace is like a boomerang; we can never out-give the Lord.

Life-Changing Verse:

Give away your life; you'll find life given back, but not merely given back—given back with bonus and blessing. Giving, not getting, is the way. Generosity begets generosity (Luke 6:38, The Message).

Life-Changing Challenge:

Give grace where you see none. Interview a difficult person or their neighbors or family to find a grace to celebrate. If you can't find something they are or something they did, then celebrate what God's Word teaches they can become. Practicing honor can change our attitudes toward others. Receiving honor often gives them hope that they can live up to what we (and God, long ago) chose to believe for them.

❧10❧
A Fear-Fighting Hug

Tears and trembling and wide-eyed fear characterized my youngest grandchildren's faces on their first visit to Children's Hospital to see their brother, David, who had cancer.

"Why are there so many cars in the parking lot, Gramma?"

When I explained that most of those cars in the hospital parking ramp represented family and friends like them who were visiting a very ill child, they were oppressed into silence. The views of children in various states of pre- and post-surgery being moved about the halls, and later meeting the children and their families, gave us a thorough education in the recognition of pain and fear. This was also the perfect opportunity to teach the children how God's love had already conquered that fear and every reason to feel fear. Feeling fear is the feeling of being out of God's arms. Using that fear as a reminder to run to His embrace helped the children cope with their natural fears regarding their own future as well as that of others.

This time I was meeting David and his mom when they returned from the hospital x-ray area. I easily found the waiting room by following a silver-haired African-American man carrying twin toddlers. He sat down and held the girls, one on each knee. One girl appeared frail and listless, but the more robust twin was crying and wouldn't allow her grandpa to comfort her.

I swear God pushed me toward her to give her a hug. I put out my arms like I would to my own child or grandchild. The man apologized that she never goes to strangers, hardly to other family members, then blinked in astonishment as she looked up, lifted her arms, and settled onto my chest, embracing me tightly.

Tenderly crooning to her, I sensed she was in need, and prayed for her peace and healing as we paced back and forth across the waiting room. The little one had stopped crying and seemed to listen to the prayers sent winging to heaven on behalf of her and her family. I thought of Nehemiah 4:14: When I saw *their fear,* I rose and spoke to the nobles, "Do not be afraid…remember the Lord who is great and awesome" (NASB, emphasis added). And so I whispered to this little one that Jesus had sent a hug through me and she shouldn't be afraid, for the Great and Awesome One was with her.

The man turned toward the elevator as a surprised grandmother exited, glancing between him and me and the now-contented little one. Simultaneously, our grandson returned from his test, and I moved to return the baby to her grandparents. A quick word of comfort regarding God's care for them and Nehemiah's prayer that I'd shared with the little girl brightened their eyes.

A nurse arrived, remarking that the child's contentment was unusual, and we turned toward the elevator. The little family waved goodbye, their thanks and blessings ringing in our ears as the elevator doors closed.

"What was that about, Gramma?" David asked, always sensitive to experiences of others. "Did you know those people?"

I shared the story of God directing me to comfort that little one, and each person's response. "Good," he whispered. "And you wouldn't have been here to do that if I didn't need these tests, would you?"

I looked into eyes that exposed an unselfish heart, once again seeing beyond its own needs. This young man, whose faith had taught me to entrust my fears to the Lord, reached around my shoulders and pulled me into him for a side hug. "I didn't realize," I teased in an attempt to keep from crying, "that a fear-fighting Jesus-hug was a boomerang."

His slow smile matched his quiet response: "Every time."

Life-Changing Lesson: All fear is conquerable.

When. If. All fear is conquerable *when* I remember Who's with me to vanquish the fear. *If* I get my focus on Him, I'll get my focus off the fear. God tells us we don't need to fear because He's with us. He reminds us what not to do (don't look anxiously about ourselves or at the circumstances) because He—God—is the conqueror. We're not trusting if we look to anything or anyone else. He says if we want to conquer fear, remember this promise: "I will strengthen you, surely I will help you, Surely I will uphold you with My righteous right hand. …But in all these things we overwhelmingly conquer through Him who loved us" (Isaiah 41:10, Rom. 8:37, NASB),

Life-Changing Verse:

The LORD is my light and my salvation; Whom shall I fear? (Psalm 27:1, NASB).

Life-Changing Challenge:

Mark a separate page in your journal for fears. List the fear; next to it, list the name of God that promises to overcome the fear. The LORD is derived from *El, God is,* the beginning of the God-names, which illuminate His character. God's character titles speak of who God *is,* not just what God *does.* For example: All God does and says is pure because God *is* purity. So when I fix my hope on God instead of the fear, those demeaning and controlling thoughts are replaced with pure thoughts (see 1 John 3:3). Some other names of God are *El (azar) Eleazar*: God is our helper—strong, powerful, almighty; *El Shaddai*: God is all-sufficient. Some resources I enjoy for a study of God's names are http://www.child-bible-lessons.com/names-of-God.html and http://www.blueletterbible.org/study/misc/name_god.cfm

Give your fears to God. Then check back a week or month later and write what happened with those fears.

11
Give Floyd $20

There was that voice again, telling me for the umpteenth time this week to give $20 to an old friend named Floyd. Trouble was, I hadn't seen Floyd or his wife, Bonnie, in some time.

The last time I'd seen Floyd and Bonnie they'd been managing an apartment complex on the north side of town. Another time, when I saw Bonnie at a gym, she said they were attending a church in another town, so I'd assumed they moved away.

I couldn't recall the church she named and I no longer attended the gym, so I prayed, "Lord, I will obey. I'll put the money in my wallet for Floyd, but I'll need you to help me find him."

Days after the envelope was readied, another old friend died in a traffic accident. Ken and I headed for the pre-funeral family visitation. The event was extremely well-attended, and we were in line for quite some time, wending our way via serpentine lines woven through the porch, halls, back, and sides of the large parlor. Finally on my way out I felt a tap on my shoulder and heard a familiar voice saying, "Hello, old friend." Bonnie, Floyd's wife, had found me, and Floyd was coming up behind her.

He seemed quite surprised when I exclaimed, "I wondered how I'd find you!" We exchanged addresses and updates then I pulled the envelope from my wallet and told Floyd how God had been "pestering me" for days with the message to "give Floyd $20." I told him I wasn't sure why or how I was going to find him, but now he was here and I was glad to present his gift from God.

The look Floyd and his wife exchanged told us there was more to the story. They soon shared a ripple-effect of unfortunate circumstances, including a second funeral out of town the following day and an empty gas tank. Bonnie told me how just that day, rather than pray for all their present needs, they simply asked God to supply what they needed for the next day. Their need for that day was funds for gas so they could attend that funeral and honor their other friend's memory.

We were blessed to be a part of that answer to prayer, and to have knowledge and contacts to suggest for other concerns of this dear couple. Bonnie was so encouraged to realize that apparently, as they were praying, God was nudging me to prepare to answer their prayer.

Life-Changing Lesson: Prepare for God to work

I need to do as God directs, and then expect God to follow through, even if I don't know the how or the when of the delivery. I also need to prepare for being God's representative. It's like preparing to sail a boat. We won't get far if we don't pull up the anchor. In this case, doubt was holding me back. Once I put the prompt into action and put the money in an envelope, God brought us together with Floyd and Bonnie.

Life-Changing Verse:

Instruct them to do good, to be rich in good works, to be generous and ready to share (1Timothy 6:18,NASB).

Life-Changing Challenge:

Ask yourself if you're ready to bless someone today. If not, do what you need to do (lift up, loosen, remove, take away any doubt, sin, reluctance, or fear that might prevent you from following God's mysterious command). If you don't have a specific direction, then practice being prepared. Pray about putting a Bible verse or a few dollars or a small gift—or all of these—in an envelope. Ask God to direct you to the needy recipient. Be patient, but be aware of those around you. Don't forget to journal your delivery adventure when you're finished, as the reminder will make the next time even easier!

12
God's Toes

My heart had been forever changed through the generosity of others providing a fundraiser for our grandson. Since that experience, I'm more than happy to contribute or to help collect for the benefit of others. For one benefit, another committee member made dozens of calls for items for the silent auction, leaving my name as the pick-up person as she had to go on vacation.

After what seemed like the hundredth stop and being constantly amazed at the merchants' kindnesses, I parked the car outside a spa. I always prayed before each visit that in addition to receiving the gift, I'd be able to leave a word, a smile, or a tangible touch of God for someone in that establishment.

Make an appointment.

The thought popped into my head, and I knew God had something in mind.

I told the receptionist I'd come to pick up the fundraiser donation but also wanted to make an appointment. I asked to see the list of services and mentally reviewed them as I read: I didn't need a haircut, and I can do a manicure at home, so I signed up for a pedicure for the following day.

I did enjoy the relaxing treatment, being pampered, and chatting with the pedicurist. But we were having only small talk, and I didn't feel any leading or needs to address. I wondered, *Could I have misread the Spirit's direction*? Just then the pedicurist said she'd be leaving the room for a few minutes while the polish dried.

The beautician stationed next to the pedicurist had been glancing over from time to time. As soon as the pedicurist left, she turned from her customer and whispered to me, "Are you Delores?" She then told me I'd sat near her at a funeral three years prior and said something that comforted her.

"I seriously need spiritual direction," she continued, "and I asked God this morning to send someone." She said she was stunned when I walked in. I, in turn, was surprised she recognized me. When I checked out, she was by the desk writing out her name and phone number. With a huge smile she accepted the material I had in my purse and promised to follow up on our contact.

I left amazed how God used my toes to put me where this gal could get to me with one quick turn and thirty seconds to whisper her request!

Life-Changing Lesson: Don't just talk to God; listen too!

God created us to represent His heart and to be His hands and feet to others. Just as we know the voice of our loved ones after spending much time with them, we can also know the voice of God.

Life-Changing Verse:

"Whether it is pleasant or unpleasant, we will listen to the voice of the LORD our God to whom we are sending you, in order that it may go well with us when we listen to the voice of the LORD our God." (Jeremiah 42:6 NASB)

Life-Changing Challenge:

Acknowledge that we will only *know* or understand the voice of God *if* we spend time in His presence. When you study your verse for today, don't just read the words and move on. Ask yourself for whom the verse was written, what the purpose was for the writing, and what direction there might be in the verse for your life. When you practice this, you're *hearing* God's words and will more readily *hear* his voice directing you. This practice leads to a dialogue of intimacy.

13
An Angelic Hug

I'd never imagined feeling peaceful and at loose ends all at the same time. Our grandson had gone to be with the Lord the night before, halfway across the country. Today was Election Day and I had committed to work the polls, but I was an emotional mess. David's cancer had spread, and we'd known for the past couple of days he wouldn't be with us much longer. One thing after another, I'd been the arranger, getting plane tickets to send the siblings and the pastor to be with them, silently crying because I wanted to go. Each time we took someone to the airport, I felt as though another bit of my heart went with them. I wanted to comfort my daughter. I wanted to be with the family. I wanted to touch my "champ" one more time.

I knew David was in good hands, I knew his faith was strong, and I knew his parents and siblings were with him, yet I felt very alone. I hadn't slept for the past several days, praying for David and his family.

I restlessly paced, reviewing all that had transpired, knowing I'd be excused if I called the election bureau but also knowing we needed the money. I wrestled with visions of bursting into tears before strangers. A last-minute call from the city helped me to decide.

I'd been reassigned to a different polling place than where I usually worked. The new place was the school where a Christian friend named Judi was employed, and I gladly accepted the change without explaining my dilemma. Perhaps I'd see Judi, and she could pray for me.

My emotions still ricocheted. I headed for the school, wondering again if I'd made a mistake promising to work that day.

The enemy began filling my mind with negative thoughts, telling me I didn't even know if Judi would be in the building that day. On my way into the school, my cellphone rang. Cellphones aren't allowed in the schools, so I paused under an entrance overhang. I was explaining the situation to a dear cousin from Florida when Judi arrived at work and overheard. She quickly promised to be praying then hurried off, indicating I could join her in the school lounge at lunchtime.

I had a tough morning emotionally, and though my coworkers were kind, heart-prayers kept flowing upward. *Lord, I need a hug or... something...*

Judi had just stopped before my table to announce her lunch hour when an unknown woman rushed toward us. Her '70s-style long hair and flowing ankle-length garments marked her as eccentric, and I turned to see where she was headed. Everyone smiled and shrugged their shoulders as the woman barreled right up to me and announced, "God thinks you need a hug, and He sent me to give you one." She engulfed me in her fluttering embrace, then reached into her purse and pulled out an angel pin. She pressed the pin into my palm saying, "Just a little reminder that God hears our prayers."

Momentarily startled into muteness, I shook my head and asked her if she'd come to vote. "No," she replied. "I came because you needed this angel today."

Her assignment completed, she fluttered away, waving and wishing us all a good election. Others said they'd seen her before but didn't know her name. Everyone seemed amazed, I most of all because no one else knew of my whispered prayer to God—no one except the woman He'd obviously told.

Life-Changing Lesson: God hears the cries of our heart.

Before I knew my need, God had planned to fill that need. Prayers aren't always long or even necessarily vocal. Many are the "heart-prayers" rising to heaven without a sound. God heard my heart-prayer that day, though unvoiced and only in my thoughts.

Life-Changing Verse:

Cast your burden upon the LORD, and He will sustain you; He will never allow the righteous to be shaken (Psalm 55:22, NASB).

Life-Changing Challenge:

What is there in your life and mine today that we need to cast out or, in other words, pitch over to the Lord? He promises to sustain us, not just from the need or burden but from ourselves. To sustain us when we're straining to do what we can't, focusing on the burden instead of the rest of our life. Can't you see the picture of us with a pitchfork in our hands, piled with burdens, and instead of picking through them and keeping some for ourselves, we just pitch them over to God. Gone. Pitched out of our hands and into the arms of our Lord, like a child handing Daddy a burden that's too heavy. When Daddy has our burden, we can no longer reach or grasp that problem. There's no string attached to allow us to pull the burden back. That's trust. I put the date I pitched over this burden next to this verse in my Bible. What will you pitch over today?

14
The Family Keys

We weren't getting any younger. My older sister and I hadn't spent time together for over twenty years. The distance of living a state apart grew smaller as we decided I'd reserve the hotels and she'd plan the itinerary for a trip together.

Due to a Packers' football game, the closest available location for Saturday was forty-five minutes north in Marinette-Menominee. Then a concert cancelled, so Marlene arranged a tour of an American Indian museum instead. Despite the setbacks, we determined to take each day's adventure as just that—an adventure.

The Menominee Reservation appeared deserted when we pulled into the parking lot Friday morning, so we headed to the building marked "office." Inside was a long table piled with huge sacks of potatoes and several gigantic pots. The women working there glanced up at us in surprise. When we explained our arrival, they apologized profusely for an apparent mix-up; tours were cancelled this morning because they were preparing for a fundraising breakfast the following day. The ladies turned back to their work, assuming we'd leave.

Sisters, as I'm sure you know, communicate without many words. After a mutual glance and a shrugging of shoulders, we surprised the women by reviewing our situation. We sisters were together for the first time in decades, we'd travelled from Green Bay, and we had several hours free. Why not stay and help? The women answered us with welcoming laughter, pushing back chairs to make room for us.

Potato peels flew as Kris, Wanda, and others shared family stories, memories of native upbringing and challenges, and then questioned us in turn. Surprised to hear our paternal grandmother was a Native American, they knew the right questions to ask of us. They also responded to our questions with "I know that name" and "The herbalist researched that…" Recognizing family names, cooking familiar herbs, and sharing similar stories of growing up in the forest made us feel at home. Hours passed with warm affirmation, and we promised to return the following morning.

Breakfast was a "lumberjack" affair, and they served us with the respect reserved for family elders. Our eyes met frequently with surprise and emotion at unexpected feelings of a reunion. Several men explained their history in forestry. We felt they were telling our story as we'd used many of the tools on display, peeling cedar and working beside our dad in his logging business. This was our heritage. We helped the women set up for cultural demonstrations; tables of handmade and donated raffle items soon filled the yard. At one point I was handed a pouch of money. I was humbled and teary-eyed at their trust, until my sister astutely pointed out that we were surrounded by several hundred full-blooded Indian Americans, and I wouldn't have gotten very far had I thought of making a run for it. A burst of women's laughter revealed we'd been overheard.

During departure hugs, they bemoaned our staying in Green Bay. They said the story of Queen Marinette (the famous female trader for whom the town and county were named) could have a key to our history, because Queen's maiden name and our grandmother's family name and place of origin were the same. But, they lamented, the book was only sold an hour north of our Green-Bay hotel, at the museum in Marinette. Our giddy sister-look drew an explanation of how our hotel got changed from Green Bay to one in Marinette—just across the bridge from the museum.

Anticipation fueled our drive, but Marinette's museum was closed for the winter. We longingly eyed books and artifacts through the window, wishing we could get in. The nearby visitor-center staff confirmed that Queen was entombed at the local cemetery, also closed on weekends. We drove there anyway, surprised to find a clerk working make-up time. She armed us with a map of plots and directions to the local printer that published Queen's story. We quickly photographed family sites then headed for the little print shop.

A friendly blond man greeted us. On the counter next to him, our cousin Mike's name on the spine of a book caught our eye. We excitedly explained the book was about our mother's family and was written by a well-respected man from the area. That information seemed to increase the printer's friendliness. When he rang up the purchase of the book, we took turns sharing the tale of our quest. He listened with a curious smile as though anticipating a punch line. What we really wanted, he sadly concluded, was Queen Marinette's story. Yes, we lamented, but that story was out of reach, behind the window of the locked museum. We asked for the ISBN number so we could order online and were stunned when he somewhat sternly refused. We stood gaping at the confusing change in him until he laughingly jingled his pocket, explaining, "There's no need because I stock the museum store…and I have the key!"

Instead of our plans being thwarted, doors that appeared closed were opened. We're still investigating the new link of our Native American history through material provided by the herbalist and the printer, but our hearts already welcomed them as family. We'd experienced the anonymous but well-known quote: "There is no key to happiness. The door is always open."

Life-Changing Lesson: God's Word is Alive

Our morning devotions—readings from the Bible—came alive each day as events revealed a cause, a quote, or a goal achieved. Don't make the mistake of reading God's Word as you would any other book. Read the Word as it is—alive! God-breathed...

Life-Changing Verse:

...For I am the LORD their God, and I will answer them (Zechariah 10:6, NASB).

It will also come to pass that before they call, I will answer (Isaiah 65:24, NASB).

Life-Changing Challenge:

Are you like me, seeking to open doors that are already opened? We thought we were running on a wild-goose chase, but before we asked, God had provided the answer.

Are you facing a challenge today? Are you ready to believe God already has the solution? One method is TTT—Tried, Tested, and found True. The Ellicot commentary explains that Isaiah 65:24 is saying God's answer anticipates our prayer...or "whatever they ask, I have an answer already prepared." Choose one of the above verses, and ask God to help you believe the verse for yourself. Now "fast" from worrying about your need by replacing doubt with thanks for what God has already prepared. When the concern comes to mind, re-read the verse and write out the words, putting your name in the verses in place of "their" and "they." When God gives you the answer, write "TTT" next to the verse: Tried, Tested, and found True.

❦15❧
Stranger No More

As Richard entered the main office of the school where I worked, his 6'4" height made him noticeable, even without his usual bright smile. I was new to this large urban high school, and hadn't yet become acquainted with all of the almost 200 staff members. I knew little of Richard besides his name and department, and that he seemed to be well-liked and respected by other staff, my co-workers, and my boss, the directing principal.

Word had gotten around that Richard suffered a sudden heart attack and had emergency surgery. He'd be away from work for some time. Speculation was that although the situation would be onerous for anyone, Richard especially would be bothered to have his activities severely limited. Coming at the end of the school year, the restrictions would be very difficult as Richard would know he couldn't participate as usual in the commencement of kids he'd helped bring to this point over the past four years.

A few days later, I was surprised to hear my boss's voice greeting

Richard. I turned curiously from the wall of mailboxes and was alarmed at Richard's lack of color. My concern rose from the obvious lack of spirit he showed when he stated he'd come to report that his doctor had ordered him to retire. Although we weren't acquainted beyond occasional greetings and generalities, when they finished their discussion, I felt compelled to step up to the counter and touch his pale hand. My tongue stumbled, and inadequacy reigned as I attempted to offer a bit of cheer. As he turned to leave, I called out, "Richard, we'll be praying for you."

He turned in the doorway and finally raised his head to meet my gaze. "Thanks," he said. "But I feel like my life is over if I can't be with the students." With that he left the building.

I was stunned, not only by his words but that he'd share such desperate thoughts with a virtual stranger amidst a crowded main office. A co-worker whispered to me, "I heard. It's so sad. His career was his life, and now it's suddenly over." We shook our heads in sorrow, and she reached for the ringing phone while I returned to my office.

For several weeks following that incident, his words "my life is over" rang in my ears. I thought about, worried about, and prayed about this man several times every day, hoping one of his friends or family would help him out of his obvious depression. As Thanksgiving vacation neared, my concern mounted. I was well acquainted with statistics of depression during major holidays, and I wondered how this season might affect Richard. Concerned but uncomfortable calling a virtual stranger, I contacted the school psychologist, who sympathized with my feelings, but told me if God gave me the burden then I'd have to make the contact. She offered to pray for me, and after we hung up, I played the scene in my mind over and over again. How might I react if a mere acquaintance from work called and asked me, "Are you depressed?" After sharing my rising panic about Richard with my husband, I had a restless night. He agreed with Jan that I should make a contact and then prayed for me to have the strength to do what was right.

The Wednesday before Thanksgiving, everyone at school was in high spirits, anticipating family time and the holiday vacation from school, but I couldn't concentrate. I tried in vain to "tune out" the message ringing in my head: *Call Richard, call Richard, call…*

About mid-morning I couldn't take the prompting anymore and asked my boss for a few moments of his time. I reviewed what I'd seen and heard of Richard, and my mounting concern for his well-being. I told him I feared Richard might hang up on me, yet I felt someone *must* contact Richard today. I was relieved that he didn't make light of my anxiety, but I felt cornered when he too agreed with the social worker's and my husband's conclusions that I must make the call. He suggested I close my office door—something I never did—and offered to prevent any interruptions.

I had tried all avenues I could think of and felt time was running out. I went into my office and closed the door. I pulled out Richard's number from the staff directory and set the paper in the middle of the desk. Then I prayed for God's guidance and for my acceptance of the outcome.

Talk about a rebel! Even as I was dialing the phone I got a final "inspiration" of how I could get out of it. I'd talk to his wife instead of Richard. *Yes, that's it*, I thought. *Woman to woman, she'd understand my concern and "watch out" for Richard.* However, I'd no sooner thought this when Richard himself answered the phone. Startled, I stuttered and asked to speak to his wife. He responded in a melancholy tone that his wife was out with the girls, picking up a few things for *her* trip to go up north to see family for Thanksgiving. They should be back in about an hour to pack up and leave. My brain felt numb with my fears for him, and though I'd suggested to others what they could say to him, I couldn't get the words out. "Okay," I replied. "I'll call back later." I hung up, disgusted with myself, my heart clenching in fear. I reviewed how he seemed to emphasize *her* trip and *they* are going, rather than *we* are going. His words seemed to echo in the room, and I was ashamed of my failure.

I prayed again and pleaded with God to take away this burden, but the cloud didn't lift. A phrase from a verse where Jesus said, "… when you give to a brother you give to me…" (Matt 25:40, NASB) came to mind. I found myself nodding my head in obedience and dialed Richard's number again. The phone rang as I mentally pleaded, *Oh, God, put the words in my mouth! Tell me what to say.* Richard's dull hello seemed to loosen a wall of emotion and memories of my Dad and how depressed he was after his heart attack.

"Richard? I called a minute ago and asked to speak to your wife because I didn't know if you'd speak with someone you barely know, but your reaction to your surgery reminded me of my daddy, and I'd like to tell you about him if you'd listen."

His soft-spoken acceptance of "Go ahead. Sure, I'll listen," led me back to Daddy's surgery.

As I told Richard how my dad loved his job and made his job his life, he said he understood. When I told him how, following a major heart attack, Daddy told me he felt like he'd never be whole again, Richard said in obvious surprise, "He felt that way, too?" I continued to share how the family felt helpless before the strange enemy of depression that literally locked Daddy away from our reach, and yet we were confident God had a plan for his life as He had for us. I shared our desperation to reach Dad and suggested perhaps Richard's wife and daughters also felt hurt as we did. I suggested they might be feeling like failures because they couldn't seem to get through to him, just as we couldn't get through to our dad.

Richard's voice slowly came to life. "Why, I never imagined they might feel that way," he said thoughtfully. "I know they love me, and I think the world of them too." Richard agreed with me as I shared John 3:16 that God loved us even more than any of our family could, and gave His Son for us to do what we could not do for ourselves. I told him that once Dad found hope in God's message, he was ready to listen to his doctor and get help for his depression.

A hopeful "Really?" came through when I told Richard the doctor said depression was a normal side-effect for many people after heart surgery and "nothing to be ashamed of." Although I was getting braver as we talked and felt the words being placed in my mouth, I was surprised at myself when I asked him to make me several promises.

I quickly requested he postpone whatever plans he had and go on the family trip for Thanksgiving. While there, I asked him to write down all he read and saw that God had done for him and given him. Finally, I requested that he call the doctor and me when he got back.

When Richard responded in a slow drawl that he did have plans of his own for that evening but he supposed he could put them off, I felt an added assurance that he'd be under his family's watchful eye until he saw the doctor. When I told him I knew I had no right as a stranger to ask him these things, there was a quiet pause and then Richard told me, "I don't think we're strangers anymore." He promised he'd report in when he got back from vacation.

I felt like singing as we hung up! I bowed my head in thanks and reviewed every nuance in Richard's voice. Was I imagining things, or had the tone changed?

The final bell of the day brought me out of my reverie, and I was surprised we'd talked so long. I looked up as my boss opened the door and asked how our conversation had gone. When I related it to him, he was astonished that I'd requested promises, but he assured me that if Richard said he'd do something, the man would keep his word.

As Thanksgiving preparations filled our home, I imagined

Richard with his family and wondered what was taking place in his heart. I wondered about him on Monday but marveled at the peace I felt. Tuesday morning the phone rang. Richard was completely different, jubilantly announcing, "You were right! The doctor said I have a side-effect from surgery, and I'm starting a prescription today as a remedy." He paused before adding that he'd "already begun the prescription you gave me" and felt his life had changed. I tearfully accepted his thanks for calling.

I thought that was the end of the story—until two weeks later when I received a card from his daughter, saying, "We don't know all of what you shared with my dad, but that conversation changed his life. We have our daddy back." To think I almost missed out on that blessing by being worried what someone would think of a stranger calling!

The next morning, I was in my boss's office checking a problem on his computer when he turned to the doorway to greet a smiling Richard.

"You see a new man before you," Richard announced, causing me to look up and smile at the sight of a healthier and more peaceful-looking man. Richard had come on a mission, however, and quickly revealed what the mission was by pointing at me and asking my boss, "Did you know about her phone call?"

"Yes, I did," he answered.

"Well, what she didn't know was that I had a gun ready that night," he said, his eyes locked on mine, "and I had plans to use it. But God told a stranger to call me and wake me up."

The three of us were locked in a moment of startled silence and reverence for God's intervention through a reluctant messenger. The words that lay closest to my heart even today came next: "But we're strangers no more."

Life-Changing Lesson: Where God leads, He empowers.

Several keys in this story reveal who I gave control to at any moment.

To tremble inwardly. To suddenly be alarmed (or agitated). To make a hasty or rash decision. None of these illustrations of anxiety are from God, and all reveal the influence and control of Satan. I had to learn to recognize fear's traps and reject them.

Life-Changing Verse:

Do not fear, for I am with you; Do not anxiously look about you, for I am your God. I will strengthen you, surely I will help you, Surely I will uphold you with My righteous right hand (Isaiah 41:10, NASB).

Life-Changing Challenge: Seek wisdom before relief.

Haven't we all done that—not taken the time to go to the Lord and ask for wisdom and direction? Quickly, rashly sometimes, we made the decisions we felt would bring the quickest relief. We can often spot the error of our ways looking back, so what can we do to change the reaction?

Promise yourself you'll ask three questions before making a decision: 1) Have I prayed about this and submitted my fear to the Lord? 2) Does my reasoning (lack of action due to fear, in this case) have a scriptural basis? 3) If the fear is true, what difference will the decision make in five years, ten, or twenty?

My issue in this instance was fear of being embarrassed. My fear seems a pitiable excuse to risk what I clearly saw as a danger to a man's life. Yet fear can cripple action. Once I (finally) sought wisdom, I found courage and instant relief. I could have been too late. Please learn from my mistakes, write out the three questions, and carry them with you. They changed my life too.

~16~
You're the One!

An overnight with my daughters at a women's conference was the incentive I needed. Preparing hearts as well as wardrobe was the agenda of the day. Praying as I packed, I asked God if I'd forgotten anything. Immediately came the direction: *You'll need $15. Fold the bills and cover the ten-dollar bill with the five. Have it ready to give to someone.*

I wonder if God didn't think sometimes He should have had me named *Yahbut*, as once again my immediate response was, "Yeah, but how will I know who to give it to?" My concern ended at the thought, *You'll know by the look on her face.*

What would you do next? I folded the bills as directed, placed them in an easily accessible spot in my purse, and began wondering what that "look" would actually look like.

Wonder, excitement, and awe abound in these experiences, but fun and laughter are nearly always present as well. I went to sleep thinking of all the possibilities God might use to bring together at least two women from different places. The truth was simpler—and more amazing—

than I could have imagined. I opened my eyes the next morning…and I knew. I'd dreamed of the woman at the conference to whom the money was directed.

God has an amazing sense of humor. He knew I'd be curious, but He also knew I had lessons to learn at the conference. He didn't want me to be distracted about the mission by trying to figure out which woman was to receive the money. Now that I'd seen her face, I wouldn't need to be looking about for direction. I could fully listen to the messages and glean the lessons God would bring through conference speaker, Liz Curtis Higgs.

Naomi, Ruth, and Boaz came to life that morning for several hundred women. We laughed, cried, and sighed as the redemptive story unfolded. During one break, I'd just had a photo taken with Liz Curtis Higgs when I heard a discussion behind me

"Oh, no! I can't believe you don't take credit cards. I so wanted to get a CD for my friend I brought to the conference."

"And for you," the friend reminded shyly.

I turned to look, and there was the girl in the dream showing a $5 bill to the clerk, saying, "This is all the cash I have." The CDs were $10, confirming the amount I'd been directed to share.

"You're the one!" I burst out then reached into my purse.

The astonished young woman turned to me as I said, "God told me to bring this and to give it to you." She reached out to my hand, seeing only the top bill, thanking me while instantly making a decision.

"Now I can send this home with my friend," she said, her eyes and voice full of meaning, significantly telling her friend she was coming first. As I left, I envisioned the clerk accepting the money from the girl and handing a CD to her friend. Instead the clerk cried out, "Wait, there's more here. You both can get one!" The girl grabbed my arm, halting my exit. "How…? What …?"

I couldn't help but laugh. "I'm just as excited as you are to be a part of God's delivering a blessing," I said. I included the friend while explaining that God loved them and must have an important message on the CD that He wanted them to hear. "Listen carefully," I encouraged.

The buzzer sounded, reminding us to return to our seats. Women laughed and cried through the skillful telling of a story most had heard a dozen times before. Ruth, Naomi, and Boaz were no longer just names. We now felt their personalities, their burdens, and their joys.

After Ms. Higgs' telling of the final chapter, my joy that day included seeing the lady who'd received the first CD join with about fifty others in responding to a call for prayer.

Usually reticent about lifting my toneless voice in public, I surprised my daughters by singing out the closing song of rejoicing. God was in our presence. Amen and amen!

Life-Changing Lesson: Truly knowing another requires active personal knowledge.

I readily recognized the woman from my dream, but I didn't really *know* her. I only knew *about* her. We can also *know about* Christ without *knowing* Him. To truly know someone literally means "to know again"—a repeated history of relationship-building. Getting acquainted takes action, trust, and time.

Life-Changing Verse:

So Jesus said, "When you lift up the Son of Man, then you will know that I am He…" (John 8:28, NASB).

Life-Changing Challenge:

Our personal relationship with God is not to be used for selfish fulfillment, but rather to be used to acquaint others with Christ. What personal knowledge have you been given about God, and how can you share that insight? Write a timeline of the past year, marking major events and the experience or knowledge you learned from each. Pray about that list, asking God to show you who needs what you've learned, and be prepared to share with them. Write a three-minute summation—what you didn't know, how God taught you, the difference the lesson made in your life—so you can simply and quickly share your experience. Ready, set, go!

17
Grace and Surely

I find not reliving that Sunday very difficult. Our second daughter, Cheri, and her five children were supposed to be a few minutes behind her husband, but hadn't yet arrived at church. Several had asked where she was when the phone rang. It was the hospital, calling to say there'd been a car accident.

Now, I'm a fixer—just ask my kids—but here was one thing Mom couldn't fix. I could help, however, so I collected Cheri's little ones from the emergency room. I walked along beside Cheri as she was wheeled away for a CAT scan, assuring my scraped and bloodied daughter that a broken tooth was the worst of the children's injuries. Nurturing, feeding, and comforting them kept me praying.

Cheri, needing only stitches and time, was soon home and resumed care of her little ones. I was grateful, but my arms felt empty. I needed to talk to the Lord.

I was praying while using the treadmill, my "stress remover." Sweat and tears poured down my face as my feet pounded out frustration. Yes, exertion was doing its part, but emotion had opened the floodgates. I knew my thoughts weren't rational, but subliminal messages from my childhood opened the doors of derision at my inability to keep my child from pain.

A wounded past left me insecure, and the certainty I was unlovable haunted me. When I married, joyfully accepting my husband's remarkable love was a step taking me closer to God. Together we believed and received the love Christ displayed on the cross. But I convinced myself that both my husband's and Christ's love were shared with me for only one reason: so I could pass those loves on to my children and others in my world. Maybe that's why I also felt responsible to do what I could to mend every hurt I witnessed.

At that moment on the treadmill, however, I was filled with thankfulness that our youngest daughter and children had survived the horrific accident a few weeks earlier. Visions constantly swirled in my subconscious: the flat-as-a-pancake car, the kind police officer confirming how "lucky" they were, and the emergency room doctor shaking his head, saying the fact that no one had been killed was "miraculous." What grace we'd been given! My feet slapping the treadmill seemed to say "Thank you, thank you, thank you…" I felt the rightness in being joyful, yet there was also a niggling unrest I couldn't name. I shook off the feeling and continued on, running and glancing at my prayer list on the treadmill's reading rack.

Petition followed praise as I moved down the list of needs and names. I reached Laurie, our oldest daughter, who lived several hours north of us. Immediately an overwhelming sense of danger and concern rose up. I glanced at the clock—10 a.m.

I immediately began to worry. Where would she be now? What was happening? Why did I have this huge burden? I had no answers. If only I could take her place…bear her pain…fill her need… I'd do anything for my child.

Weeping before God to release my daughter from whatever danger she was in, I pleaded, "God, give her Your presence now. Surround and protect her, and let me bear the difficulty. Let me take her place, fill her need, no matter the consequences."

I felt a love flowing through me to my daughter wherever she was. Whatever was happening, this love was more powerful, protective, obedient, and sacrificial than I'd ever known. I gasped because deep within I heard God speaking a gentle message: *Now you understand; this is how much I love you.*

I waited for a call the rest of the day, but it never came. I don't know why I didn't call Laurie, but somehow I knew the story wasn't finished. Later I'd be glad I didn't know how my prayer would be answered.

Busy hands calm the mind, and so Ken helped me clean my little silver Toyota from bumper to bumper. We scrubbed, polished, and fixed a few things we'd been meaning to get to. I felt good the next morning, driving the freshly detailed car to work. Only two blocks away from my destination, amid an unmarked intersection, I saw danger coming—a red car, larger than mine. I knew there was no way either of us would stop in time.

Brake! My mind heard the command. Tires squealed. The red car halted after we struck, but my car spun completely around, smacked sideways against the curb, and finally stopped, facing backward in the street.

Neither of us was hurt. The other driver went on to school, but my poor little car was dented everywhere. The insurance man confirmed the car was totaled, but he said if I knew someone who'd want the car for parts, they'd reimburse the Blue-book value less the few hundred the car was now worth. We immediately thought of Laurie's husband because Doug was skilled at car repair. I called, and when Laurie answered, I blurted out, "Where were you at ten o'clock yesterday morning? What happened? Why didn't you call?"

"Ten o'clock?" I could hear the shock in her voice, followed by a drawn-out "Umm…" confirming my inner knowledge. "I didn't want to worry you, Mom," she said, then went on to confess that her car slid into the ditch and rolled over. She was unhurt, and fortunately a volunteer fireman was driving behind her and helped pull out the wrecked vehicle, but her car needed to be replaced. She asked how I knew something had happened, so I shared the story of my prayer-time premonition, and my morning. Would Doug want to repair the Toyota? He did.

Meanwhile Ken insisted he'd find a different, *safer* car for me that same night. Despite the reputation of being wheeling-dealing bargain-hunters who took time to name our cars, Ken walked into the lot and told the dealer he was sure the car we parked next to was the one. After the test drive, I offered to wait a day while Ken thought about the vehicle, or at least checked prices, but he gave his reasons, concluding, "Surely, this is the one."

"Surely?" I repeated, "As in surely goodness and mercy…"

"…shall follow you all the days of your life," he finished, laughing. We christened the car "Surely."

We left a bemused but happy salesman and drove home to meet Laurie and Doug, who'd come to pick up my little silver wreck. Cheri and her family also came to admire my pretty blue car. While the guys attached the wounded Toyota to the tow-bar, the women marveled over our three accidents in less than a month, and how much everyone had escaped.

Chuckles followed a grandchild's asking who Shirley was, and Ken's explanation of our new car's name. Our laughter turned to tender tears when Laurie gave me a hug goodbye and whispered, "I've already named my new car, Mom. She's Grace."

We'll never know the whys of those accidents, but we do know that Grace lasted just long enough for them to save up for another used car. We still have Surely, followed by God's goodness and mercy…and a very personal understanding of God's agape love.

Life-Changing Lesson: God is the fixer…not me.

All and more I think I'd do for my child, God has already done for me. I realized that just as I love my children (not for what they do or have), so God loves me. My desire to fix things for my children, which I'm sure they sometimes consider a handicap, I now see as an extension of God's care for me.

Life-Changing Verse:

Give thanks to the God of heaven, For His lovingkindness is everlasting (Psalm 136:26, NASB).

Life-Changing Challenge:

Everlasting contains both antiquity and futurity, from beginning to end. God's loving-kindness to you began before you were born, and it will extend into eternity. As you find King David's twenty-six evidences of God's lovingkindness in Psalm 136, relate each to a time in your life when God showed loving-kindness by conquering, creating, leading, guiding, remembering, rescuing, or loving you.

18
Hummer of a Day

I will never forget the sight of our fourteen-year-old grandson, Dave, being violently sick from his first round of chemotherapy. That single snapshot in time hovered like a dark cloud even though his mom later found a remedy to control the nasty side-effects. His extreme nausea represented the reality of an unexpected diagnosis—cancer in his right leg. He was home now between chemos, and today was my day with Dave.

A husky about-to-be high school freshman, Dave's pre-cancer interests had focused entirely on sports and activities. How, I wondered, would I find something to do on this cool fall day, with a young man on crutches, weakened and tired but still game for his turn to spend a day with Gramma? All past outings and ideas were scratched due to his limited strength. We'd have to find something to do for an hour or two then return home for medication before continuing. I was baffled.

Dave's eyes gleamed full of anticipation as his mom knelt to tie the shoe on his splint-protected leg. I had no idea how to fulfill that expectation. I prayed frantically for an idea, silently asking, *God, what do teenage boys like Dave want to do?* All eight grandkids had enjoyed my past spontaneity, but this time I felt hollow. Then, just as Dave asked, "What are we going to do today, Gram?" the answer came. Cars! Boys like cars...

"It's a surprise, Dave," I smiled, now calm. "I think you'll enjoy this."

We drove to Highway 20, which is lined with car dealers. Pausing expectantly before we turned on the street, Dave eyed me curiously.

"So, Dave," I said, "see any cars you want to test-drive?"

Widened eyes of shock turned quickly to a happy smirk. He chose a Cadillac, and we swung into their lot and parked. A flight of stairs led to the office, so Dave waited while I went inside.

My nephew Kenny calls me *General D* when I get this determined. I chuckled as I climbed the stairs, wishing I'd called ahead. Fortunately our arrival was at a quiet moment, and the manager who greeted me was also a grandparent. A brief explanation that I was in no position to actually purchase a car but was requesting a ride for my grandson produced a welcome, "No problem."

The manager came out and greeted Dave eagerly. "I think I have an idea which car you'd be interested in," he said, pointing out a blue sporty model.

A responsive grin, followed by the first of many sighs of "Sweet!" indicated full agreement.

Our butter-smooth ride through town was highlighted when Dave suggested we go by the house and show the family what we'd found. Everyone *oohed* and *aahed* over the features, and his siblings hinted recklessly for their next outing. After bringing the Cadillac back and giving profuse thanks, we returned home for Dave's medication. Eighteen-year-old Mike greeted him with, "After that, what'll you do this afternoon—test-drive a Hummer?"

"Yeah," Dave laughed, adding, "in my dreams." But I tore out of their house before I heard any more. The day was half over. Could we? I raced to my house and the Internet then punched in Hummer. A yelp of joy brought my husband running. There was a dealership only forty minutes away! I called with trepidation, explaining I wasn't in the market to buy the vehicle and certainly had no intention of test-driving it myself.

"Come on in!" laughed the enthusiastic manager and gave careful directions.

A few minutes later Dave was eager and ready to leave, wondering where we were going next. "A surprise in a half-hour," was all I could trust myself to say. On the way we chatted about the Cadillac ride and other cars he thought were "sweet."

The final exit was on a hill, and the Hummer showroom was visible at the bottom. "You didn't!" he said, gazing at me a moment and then back at the yellow and black signage. "I don't believe it."

In awe, we walked up the ramp to the futuristic building. Two men stood dwarfed behind massive glass doors, which apparently could open, allowing the gigantic vehicles to be driven out. We were greeted by the manager and a salesman with military-like posture. They gave Dave the royal treatment, including a tour, history of the Hummer, and a look inside standard and luxury models, before going outside for a ride.

Our guess that the erect, crewcut salesman had been a serviceman was confirmed as he guided us to the silver Hummer he'd purchased after post-military use. Gallantly hoisting Gramma into the back, they circled the Hummer admiringly and climbed in to inspect and discuss every minutiae from the rotating gun atop the vehicle to every dial and engine part. Usually bored with such guy stuff, time flew as I watched Dave's grin broaden time and again. Mike asked, "Ready for a ride?"

Dave turned, and I knew the look he flashed me would hold a lifetime of memories.

Oh, what a ride! Several times Mike or Dave would glance back and inquire if Gramma was doing okay. Gripping the seat stiffly, I did *not* enjoy riding up—or down—the 90-degree hills, but I was here for Dave and squeaked out "fine" to their chuckles. Mike drove over and through every imaginable obstacle and finished with a road test on the freeway.

Back in my own safe vehicle at last, I marveled at the answer to prayer. An exhausted Dave had placed his souvenirs and crutches in the back and tilted his seat for a rest. The quiet ride home was broken a few minutes later with a sleepy chuckle and music to a grandmother's ears: "You'll never be able to top this, Gram. It was a Hummer of a Day!"

Life-Changing Lesson: God answers when I *need* it, not when I *want* it.

God may not answer my prayers until the moment I *need* that answer, but I know He *will* answer. Don't be tempted to play the bargaining game with God. Be direct, ask Him for what you need, and expect the answer when you need it.

I certainly made a desperate cry for help that day. Though I know in my heart God was aware of the need before I presented it, He wanted me to trust that He's working even when I can't see the work-in-progress, and especially when I can't do anything about it myself. (I tend to do what I can about a situation and then ask God when I run out of my own ideas.) I need to make a practice of asking God first.

Life-Changing Verse:

"Call to me and I will answer you. I'll tell you marvelous and wondrous things that you could never figure out on your own" (Jeremiah 33:3, The Message).

Life-Changing Challenge: Ask God for a solution.

Next time you find yourself faced with a perplexing question, early on—*before* you try to find the answer yourself—ask God for a solution. Psalm 5:3-NASB says, "In the morning [early] O LORD, You will hear my voice; In the morning [early] I will order my prayer to You and eagerly watch" (bracketed emphases mine).

After asking, write down the need in your journal. Go about your day expecting God to work, and write in His response later. This is a great practice of trust, and a great reminder to look back and see how many times and ways God has answered prayer.

～✥19✥～
An Angel for Heaven

Mesmerized, I reached for the brown-skinned cloth doll on the museum gift shelf. Its tag, "I'm Angel and I'm washable," made her perfect for a toddler. Though I had no idea for whom the doll was intended, I knew the colorfully-dressed, dark-braided treasure was coming home with me.

Two years later, I was still praying for the child God meant to receive Angel.

For months I took out the doll, prayed for her recipient, scanned the birthday list, and put her back. On several trips, Angel went in my suitcase, but always came back. Eventually I rewrapped the doll and tucked her away on the closet shelf.

Retirement was coming and I entertained co-workers with countdowns of every variety, including a mission-trip goal. Samaritan's Purse's request for help cleaning abandoned homes months after hurricane Katrina was perfect timing; we'd head for New Orleans the first day of my retirement.

Boots and throw-away clothes were recommended gear for gutting mud-filled homes and clearing fallen trees for senior citizens living in temporary mobile quarters. Reaching into the back of the closet, I once again tucked Angel in the suitcase.

Thirteen hours of driving later, the college students and I fell into beds three hours from our destination. Early the next morning, as we completed the last leg of our trip, we got the shock of our lives. A growing sea of blue-tarped roofs led us to devastation as surreal as a holocaust movie set. Smashed cars wrapped around poles and pilings under the interstate; huge trees had fallen and splintered homes and vehicles. Every fence and building had a yellow line from the water and sewage, marking the depth of cataclysmic events. Orange federal codes marked windows: search date, and number of people and animals found dead or alive. How eerie.

Covered from head to foot in white sanitation coveralls, respirators, gloves, and boots, we stood outside the community center to get equipment for each job. We were given chainsaws, shovels, rakes, wheelbarrows, hammers, and crowbars. We soon knew why. One senior's house, uninhabitable due to mold, had big six-inch water and sewer pipes cutting across the driveway and yard to a temporary trailer home. We sawed the fallen trees in the backyard, and hauled twisted sheets of aluminum and contents from the flattened shed. Dragging sodden refuse over the pipes to the street was exhausting, but we managed some levity in the midst of it.

I was lifting cement blocks into a wheelbarrow when our youth worker, Bryan, asked what was moving inside the block. First thinking he was teasing, I shuddered when he pointed out two spiders the size of my palm exiting the block I'd just put down. Still laughing at my reaction, Bryan reached under the tangle of warped aluminum panels and exclaimed that something felt very soft. Usually things were expectedly heavy due to water-logging, so several guys lifted the panel and revealed Bryan's hand wrapped around the neck of a possum!

At night we shared stories with other workers. I glanced around the cavernous community bedroom, wondering if Angel would go home with one of the workers, but I still had no leading.

Days later we were assigned a small, one-story, white-board home with a yellow waterline just below the roof. Water had lifted household goods to different rooms, a refrigerator had come to rest on top of other furnishings, and outside items had entered where a tree smashed a hole through the wall.

We stacked salvageable items on a bench on the front lawn, while the inside was gutted. Saved were the bench, music CDs, glass gifts still in Styrofoam containers, and wine goblets hanging in racks above the kitchen sink. A few partially-ruined pictures and two purses of coins were discovered in the master-bedroom closet. We cried with the owners when they confirmed those few items were all that remained from the history of their marriage.

They invited us to visit their father's home the next day and then join them at the French Quarter flea-market, where we'd try beignets (square doughnuts piled with powdered sugar).

We were so touched the next morning to meet the grandfather, recuperating from his narrow escape in a hospital bed set up in the living room. The father left the room to awaken their little girl, while the mother shared the horror of recognizing her home on television, amidst the rising water, and answered our question that yes, many things had yet to be replaced. My heart beat faster when her list included their two-year-old daughter's toys...including a doll.

We knew from the crib we'd pulled out of the house that they had a child, but we hadn't heard her name. We felt an unexpected joy when they introduced a sweet little girl whose name was Heaven.

I quickly reached in my bag and pulled out Angel. When I handed Angel to Heaven, the child's eyes lit up with joy. Heaven held her new toy close, while I told her parents the story of when I'd purchased the doll, unknowingly, for a little girl just being born in New Orleans.

Amidst the toil and tears of New Orleans, I experienced a highlight worth waiting two years, four days, and thirteen hours—witnessing God's love extended to a little girl by bringing Angel to Heaven!

Life-Changing Lesson: **Waiting passionately is an active role.**

What do you do when you have to wait? Don't make the mistake of thinking of waiting as doing nothing. Passionate waiting is not passive or hidden. Such waiting is active, visible, and constant. The picture I envision is someone writhing in immense pain, waiting for the painkiller. Strong's Concordance defines waiting as "very watchful, extremely eager, and restlessly watching and waiting, noticing every sound or movement that might hint at the expected and hoped-for relief." In other words, waiting is actively stepping back and letting God be God.

Life Changing Verse:

God proves to be good to the man who passionately waits, to the woman who diligently seeks (Lamentations 3:25, The Message).

Life-Changing Challenge: **Wait passionately!**

Journaling can help while watching and waiting. Looking back on what I've seen and heard (and rejected as not matching with God's Word) has proven not only to sharpen the skill of defining God's voice and direction, but also provided peace in the waiting.

This week, list a few things you're waiting for, and next to each item, note your active, passionate efforts of waiting (praying, watching, testing, listening). Leave space to record how you found something to be or not be God's voice, or God's time.

20
God's Good Spirit

September 10th is the anniversary of when my husband and I met, and that particular year our usual plans to celebrate were overshadowed by an ominous feeling of danger that I tried desperately to keep to myself. First, I suggested we cancel original plans and stay home on Monday the 10th and Tuesday the 11th. Although Sunday was a gray, rainy day, Ken was determined to celebrate in some small way, so we headed toward a Frank Lloyd Wright home about ninety miles west.

In the car, I read to Ken from a paperback titled *Names of the Holy Spirit.* We discussed Nehemiah 9:20, which says, "You gave your good spirit to instruct them," but the unsettling aura increased. Hiding anything when you've been with someone for forty years is nigh unto impossible, and as I strained to hear or see what I felt was approaching as we drove along, I stole frequent glances at the horizon. I knew my unrest hadn't gone unnoticed when Ken's soft questions, "What is it? What's bothering you?" forced me to crack a small, tight smile.

"I don't know yet," was my honest answer as I nervously glanced out my side window again. Ken questioned if we should turn back, and I hesitantly confessed to an eerie feeling that something ominous, something dark and evil was going to happen soon. I didn't know what I was feeling or watching for, but I felt the intuition coming from an area I pointed to outside the passenger window, toward the northeast.

We couldn't pull over because the rain was forceful, so we began to pray through our concerns, listing family and loved ones as they came to mind. When we arrived at Trinity's and Larry's names—our niece and her husband—I became overwhelmed with concern for them. They live in New York, far from where we were, and I'd visited them only once. My sister Marvel and her husband, William, had called from Florida a few days previously and told how they'd had a family reunion, including Trinity, Larry, and their little daughter, Autumn Lea. They'd mentioned some tidbits from the book of Revelation about coming times of peace or fear, depending on one's relationship with the Lord. As we now mused over this conversation, our mutual concern for their spiritual and physical wellbeing seemed to mount. We continued to pray for them off and on during our trip that day, over lunch, and on the return home.

I thought of calling Trinity, but feared my dark worries might seem silly, so I decided to leave my fears with the Lord. The next day my concern grew hourly. I didn't sleep that night—September 10th—praying around the list of our family and ministries, frequently coming back to Trinity and Larry.

Several times in the past, I've awakened with a need to pray for family or friends in the States or overseas and later learned of a particular need at the exact time. I wondered what physical or spiritual need Trinity and Larry could be facing to have such an unusually compelling control over my heart and mind. I determined to make a call the next day to see if there was anything I could do. I had my sister's number with me and intended to call her to get Trinity's number. I found keeping my mind on my work difficult due both to lack of sleep and the early hour. Knowing the hour was different on the East Coast, I glanced frequently at the clock to determine the best time to call. Each time I checked the time, I prayed for them again, mystified at the continued feeling of oppression and darkness.

At 9:15 a.m., I was called to the outer office. Staff had gathered under a small wall-mounted monitor, where the news of the attack on the World Trade Center was being televised.

I instantly understood the previous forty-eight hours of turmoil. Larry worked near the World Trade Center and frequently stopped at a coffee shop there on his way to work. I ran to my office and called my sister. Without a hello she answered, "Larry and Trinity are okay. He hadn't left for work yet." Then she shared the rest of the story. Trinity and Larry had planned a little family outing at the mall beneath the World Trade Center prior to Larry's scheduled work time. They planned to take the subway there, have breakfast, then shop before he went to work.

The evening before, their usually happy baby had several brief periods of fussiness with no obvious illness or reason for her behavior. They finally got to sleep in the early morning hours and consequently overslept.

Awakened by a call from Larry's mother, they rushed to the television and saw the same horrific scene I was viewing. Their eyes met with one unspoken thought: *We would have been there!*

My sister said when she saw the news and called them they were understandably shaken. She assured them God had kept them from harm. Trinity told her, "We believe, Mom. We believe!" My sister was astounded as I shared the prayer vigil for them the previous nights. We, too, believe God has a plan for them and spared them at that time.

We thank God that his Good Spirit instructed us to pray for them, not just on those days but in the days to come as well. As we look back into those verses in Revelation, we know things have only begun to happen. We must continue to pray with the same immediacy and concern for all mankind. This situation brought back recent memories when a dying friend told me, "At times like these, only two things are important: my relationships with my God and my family."

Luke 21:36 (NASB) aptly expresses it this way: "But keep on the alert at all times, praying that you may have strength to escape all these things that are about to take place, and to stand before the Son of Man."

…and God's Good Spirit will guide you.

Life-Changing Lesson: Prayer must be the first defense.

Many biblical characters reacted as we do when something happens, or when we fear something might happen. They reacted with worry, stress, anxiety, murmuring, withdrawal, confusion, fear, running, or a host of other unhealthy and unhelpful things. Statistics show that only after running the gamut of mental and emotional reactions do most people finally, as a last resort, turn to prayer and cry for help.

Life-Changing Verse:

But keep on the alert at all times, praying that you may have strength to escape all these things that are about to take place, and to stand before the Son of Man (Luke 21:36, NASB).

Life-Changing Challenge: Practice praying before reacting.

The Oxford Dictionary defines alert as "quick to notice any unusual and potentially dangerous or difficult circumstances. The state of being watchful for possible danger."

We must practice making prayer the first action and reaction to all of life's circumstances.

In Nehemiah 9, the writer lists a host of reminders of God's past actions and provisions. This produces encouragement that what God has done before, He will do again. In your journal, repeat the exercise. List things God has done for you, including—if you can remember—how God's Spirit guided you through each event. Beginning today, write out your greatest concern, and ask God for guidance to maneuver through it. Leave space to fill in guidance received and eventual resolution. I found this a life-changing practice.

✵21✵
Not Now

Each time I travel, the first thing I pack is provision for a blessing—usually funds to treat a person or family to dinner. Sometimes I also feel led to bring a book or other items. I always try to have the note or paid bill presented after I leave. I believe a gift from God should not have a face, but sometimes God shows me differently. This was one of those times.

I joined my daughter at a conference in the south for a working vacation. I'd spent most of the day researching and writing in our room while she attended meetings. Then we'd go out together in the evening.

All week I'd glance around in restaurants and at tourist stops, wondering who I could bless, but I didn't get the call to pass on a blessing.

Time flew, and on the last hours of the last day, the summons finally came. Checkout time was during the conference, so we had to bring out the luggage by 7 a.m., to be held until Laurie finished her last meeting at 12:45. Two bus routes to the airport provided rides, but since the first bus was scheduled to leave at the same time the conference ended, we planned for the second departure, half an hour later. Claim tickets in hand, Laurie dashed off to her meetings, as I noticed a young couple and baby by the bus. The soldier-husband was leaning over, kissing the baby in the woman's arms. I knew they were the ones. I took a step forward, but God whispered, "Not now."

I turned away, wondering how I was to find them again, as they appeared to be leaving. I even thought I must have misunderstood that the blessing was for them, and God would show me someone else.

A secluded bench by the pond provided a private place for me to sit and to pray for the couple, for the blessing yet to be given, and for our trip back. I was impressed at that point to give a different amount than planned, so I set the money aside thinking, *Okay, it's ready. But for whom?*

The rest of the morning was spent in delightful relaxation—walking, swinging in a hammock while finishing a paperback, and taking photos.

The chime of my cellphone signaled the conference had ended. Laurie and I took a few minutes to find each other, get to the luggage hold, and claim our bags. Surprisingly, the first bus was still there. The driver stood on the steps into the bus and asked if we'd accept the only two seats remaining, at the back of the bus. We agreed and climbed on, toting computer cases and purses sideways down the aisle to the two empty seats in the last row.

An adorable baby played peek-a-boo in the space between the two seats in front of us. The mother turned, apologetically hoping the baby wasn't bothering us. Recognizing her pretty outfit, I asked if she was the woman I'd seen with a soldier by a bus this morning. She said yes, he was going back to Iraq now that they'd had a wonderful R&R together. I told her God led me to give her a little gift, along with a pamphlet containing the story my grandson David asked me to share before he passed away in 2008.

She asked a few questions about Dave, his cancer, and his faith, and said she hoped I didn't mind entertaining the baby through the seats while she read Dave's story. I was happy to help, as the first leg of the trip flew by.

At the first terminal stop, the young mother stood to her feet and leaned toward me, offering a tearful hug. She explained that the gift met a specific need, and was the nicest thing anyone had ever done for them. I affirmed the gift was from God, and I was as excited as she that God would use me to tell them He loves them and wants to bless them. I asked for first names so I could pray for them. Then she asked if she could e-mail me later to explain how the timing and amount of the gift so amazingly fit something her husband had asked her to get.

That morning when I turned from seeing her by the bus, I couldn't understand how I'd have another opportunity to help this young couple. When God whispered, "Not now," I should have realized He'd already planned out the perfect time and circumstances of the delivery.

Our original plan when we first arrived for the conference was for Laurie to drop off her luggage alone while I finished a project, and then we'd meet after the conference. But I had translation issues with documents I planned to research that morning, so Laurie convinced me to turn in my suitcase with hers and then relax. I'd gotten a lot done, so I didn't feel too guilty taking a morning off, even though I wouldn't have if the translation problem hadn't occurred. But after sitting behind the mother and child on the bus, I understood why God had arranged for me to be where I was at exactly the right time.

I love when I get to see the reasons behind a little mission. Now I was eager to get home, where I was sure I'd find an e-mail from my new friend.

Life-Changing Lesson: Love responds with trusting obedience.

We recognize the voices of those we love, and we trust their words because they love us. When we know and respect the person speaking, we're better able to respond immediately without worry of reprisal. Reacting instead of responding reveals a lack of trust.

Life-Changing Verse:

"Do you not know that when you present yourselves to someone as slaves for obedience, you are slaves of the one whom you obey, either of sin resulting in death, or of obedience resulting in righteousness?" (Romans 6:16 NASB)

Life-Changing Challenge: Respond to God's instructions with attention and action.

Our instinct is do everything now, but the purpose of every mission is to bring God glory. Be listening for God's specific direction, and be sure to point the receiver to the *real* giver by giving God the glory. Memorizing God's Word (a verse a month is a good goal) helps us to recognize His voice. I also enjoy marking my Scripture-reading with an A by the action the verse suggests. The action might be something to do, not do, or start or stop doing, but the A will help you give attention to the words every time you open that page. What are the needed actions implied in the verse above? Note these as you journal, and list how you can fulfill each action in your daily life. That simple effort can increase the intensity of your attention to God's Word and help you to remember the verses too.

22
Sunrise Smoothies

A major health concern is always a major financial concern, and our grandson Dave's cancer was no exception. He and I were in Arizona for integrative treatment. In addition to providing transportation, Gramma's responsibility was to feed him as naturally and nutritionally as possible. Cooking from scratch takes a lot of time, and we were thrilled to find a couple of health-food stores that carried wholesome, prepared foods.

The expense of those foods, however, made their enjoyment a rarity. Dave loved to eat; consequently food became one of the focal points of his daily devotion and prayer-time requests (for Gramma to hear and hopefully answer). A favorite treat was a fruit smoothie called Sunrise, and he'd once again requested the $4 drink. Delaying the budget explanation, I put him off with a "We'll see."

Private accommodations would be available the next day, so this was our last day at the hotel with a pool. David longed to relax by the pool even though we knew radiation and some forms of chemotherapy could make patients more sensitive to the sun, especially if in the reflective water. Dave was tired of feeling like he was hiding out and tired of wearing long pants in the hot weather. He reasoned he'd limit his exposure if he wore basketball shorts, which cover more than swimming trunks, and if we went out right after breakfast before it got too hot. His eyes pleaded with me for "just a few minutes" in the sun. Of course, Gramma capitulated.

On our way poolside, Dave teased about the sunrise I'd taken him to see and photograph in Sedona, Arizona. A native jewelry display on the lookout hill sidetracked me, and Dave ended up taking the pictures while I selected souvenirs. He never let me forget that time and was again teasing me as we entered the gated pool and patio area to stretch out on the loungers in the sun.

A dark-haired woman was entering the same time as us, and she turned when Dave stated he'd never miss a sunrise, especially if it was "the kind you can drink" (hint, hint, Gramma). The lady gave him an odd look, but I figured it was due to the huge scars that ran up Dave's leg. She asked if he'd had surgery, and when he told her about the cancer, she got teary-eyed. We introduced ourselves—the woman's name was Susan—and chatted about family a few minutes, until the time came to begin our busy schedule. When Dave stood up to go, she addressed him, asking about his comment to drink a Sunrise. A big grin split his face and he said, "Yeah, a Sunrise Smoothie. Have you ever had one?"

"As a matter of fact, yes," Susan replied, grinning. She then told us she was the trainee-manager for the deli that sold Dave's favorite drink. "Any time after ten today, show them this card and you'll get a free Sunrise Smoothie—every day—as long as you're here."

"Wow, thanks!" Dave responded as they high-fived. "You're the answer to my prayer this morning." He explained to the tenderhearted manager that this was our last day at that address but that we'd be nearby for the next couple of weeks. He then exclaimed how he was so glad he hadn't missed her. She in turn said she'd never been told she was an answer to prayer and found it a rather nice feeling.

Dave wrote a thank-you note, anticipating seeing Susan to get his after-appointment Sunrise Smoothie. Susan seemed appreciative and promised to read the note. She said she'd been thinking of him as well, and surprised him again, by handing us not only the smoothies, but a gift-card for lunch in the deli.

Throughout the rest of our two weeks, Dave enjoyed the free smoothie card to the max. When we didn't see Susan during our next several visits, we asked about her and were told that the first day we came in and received the free smoothie card was her last day of working there. She'd left a message of good-bye and thanks for the inspiration.

Sunrise Smoothies were the topic of our discussion that evening. We prayed for the tenderhearted woman that God ministered to through Dave and his love for a fruit smoothie, and we gave thanks for His provision of the tasty treat.

Life-Changing Lesson: While being a blessing, you get a blessing.

Being a blessing and getting a blessing are not trade-offs, like getting a blessing as the result of your actions; the two types of blessing are simultaneous benefits of being a child of God. You *will* be a blessing—not might be, or could be, but *will* be.

Life-Changing Verse:

You'll be a blessing and also get a blessing (1 Peter 3:9, The Message).

Life-Changing Challenge: Expect to be a blessing because you bring Christ into the situation.

God says you *are* a blessing and *will* bless others, not because of what you do but because of who you are in Christ. Write out these words: I (fill in your name) will be a blessing. Now for the hard part: make a list of those who've mistreated you, and pray for them. "Bless those who curse you, pray for those who mistreat you" (Luke 6:28, NASB).

23

Love Lifted Me

Moses' arms got tired, Gideon and his men were bone-tired, David spoke to 200 of his men who were too tired to continue, and Rebekah told Isaac she was tired of living. I wasn't quite *that* tired, but I was exhausted. Exhaustion sounded like such a good excuse. If those spiritual patriarchs got tired and God understood, surely He'd understand my tiredness too. I'd barely slept the last three nights as I'd prepared material for a Christian writers' conference, and on the plane I just wanted to sleep.

Usually before I left I'd pray for an opportunity to minister to someone, but not this time. Morning would be here in a few hours. Yawning, I dropped the last papers into my carry-on next to the bed. The phone rang. It was my sister Marvel.

"I know you leave early tomorrow for your conference, and I want to pray for you before you leave," she announced as I tried unsuccessfully to hide another yawn. "You sound so tired," she added.

Smirking, I knew God was up to something. I was shaking my head at God's mysterious ways when she launched in with exactly what I'd neglected or refused to pray: asking God to lift my tiredness and give me energy and excitement for opportunities to share the Lord on the way out and on the way back. She used the word "lift" at least four times—enough so the word was my first thought on waking the next morning.

I settled in to a window seat on the plane, rebelliously grateful when seemingly everyone in line had trickled past me, leaving both seats next to me empty. One last review of materials and then a welcome nap—or so I thought. I'd finished the second of five folders when a broad-shouldered, muscular man set a small bag on the seat between us and slid into the aisle seat. We acknowledged one another with a brief hello, but still reluctant to communicate, I went back to my work. Leaning over to slide the last folder into my bag, I noticed him reaching for his laptop and thought, *Good! He'll be busy, and I can nap.*

"Looks like you're heading for some type of conference," he commented.

"Yes, a Christian Writers' Conference."

"Oh? That sounds uplifting. What type of things do you write?"

Uplifting. Huh. Interesting choice of words. My sister is going to get a kick out of this. I smiled at the inclusion of her oft-repeated word and felt a release in my soul as I gave up the napping plans to God, for whatever He had in mind.

I explained to the construction worker—whom I'll call Tom—that I wrote inspirational stories and articles about things God had done in my life, to encourage others in their search for peace and satisfaction.

He replied, "Well, isn't it interesting that I should sit next to you? Because you might say I'm kind of on a quest for God."

Wow. He had my attention! He went on to list all the books, CDs, and DVDs he'd reviewed about God, the Bible, and all types of religion and beliefs on creation. I challenged him that rather than read all those books *about* the Bible, to just read the Bible and ask God to let His words speak for themselves. He agreed but had some specific questions about the Bible—some I was able to answer, and one I promised to send a response to when I got home.

"Any conclusions from all that research?" I wondered aloud. He laughingly said that sometimes the material was so confusing he was tempted to be an atheist, but there was something inside him that made him know there's a God. He thought that inner *something* might be there because he was a builder and had designed and constructed things, so he recognized the amazing detail and design in creation.

We talked for the entire flight, and I agreed to keep in touch and, of course, to pray for him. I sent the promised answer to his question as soon as I got home, and I received a kind thank-you note back. He said he felt it was no accident that we sat together on that flight, and that he felt our conversation was an important part of his spiritual journey.

I thought of him and prayed for him often. Almost a year later, in a class about explaining some of those hard questions we'd discussed, I felt a nudge to send a copy of the book we were studying to Tom.

The Internet is a wonderful thing. Minutes after I got home, the order was placed and would be sent directly to my down-south friend. Days later I got an amazing card from Tom. His wife had passed away unexpectedly, and he was burdened with grief. He said he was in his office alone and so overcome he bowed his head and cried out, "God, are you there?" Just then the mail was delivered, and my order and "thinking of you" note was placed on his desk. He was touched at God's hand in the timing, and I was amazed that I'd even considered missing such a marvelous blessing for a nap.

We continue to keep in touch, and have had other encouraging God-led answers to prayer winging their way almost border to border. Come to think of it, I believe I'll write him a note tonight.

Life-Changing Lesson: Yielding my weakness allows God to work.

Not until we put our hand out can another pull us up. Surrendering my weakness gives God room to work and takes the pressure off of me to *fix* everything…and everyone.

Life-Changing Verse:

For if either of them falls, the one will lift up his companion. But woe to the one who falls when there is not another to lift him up (Ecclesiastes 4:10, NASB).

Life-Changing Challenge: Be willing to be the receiver; accept another's lifting up.

I recognized my sister filled this role when she called me just before I left for my flight for the conference, to bear my exhaustion, to pray for me that I'd once again be in the proper position, ready to receive God's hand and be used of Him.

When another sees a need you didn't or wouldn't see, it's a humbling experience. It encourages you to do or not do something. They, then, are being the hands and feet of God to you. Write a thank-you note today to someone who at some time in your life was your "lifter."

24
Here Am I—Bring Me

I was my mom's long-distance caregiver for several years, and her harsh and demanding personality made my friends joke that I should charge them to come with me to help her. Their reasoning was that prior to the trip to the next state, they thought their family was the most dysfunctional. But after time with my mom, they brought home strong assurance that their family wasn't so bad after all.

I'd just completed an arduous journey re-hiring Mom's in-home help after she fired them and accused them of all sorts of impossible things like stealing her double-bed through the standard-sized bedroom window. I was relaxing with a book in our study when the phone rang, and I was informed Mom had a stroke. Fortunately the in-home help was present and had arranged transportation to the hospital. I told them I'd leave within the hour. I hung up and walked into the kitchen to tell my husband, forgetting that my friend Nancy was there to explain a new church project to him.

Nancy looked up and said, "I couldn't help but hear you, and I'd love to come along and help any way I can." I hadn't known Nancy long and wasn't sure how she'd react to Mom, or how her husband might feel if we were gone several days, depending on what needs arose.

I voiced my concerns, but she quickly assured me that her own mother was a tough case, so she was confident she could handle Mom.

She quickly called her husband to explain, while I refreshed the still-packed overnight bag and tossed in a plastic slipcase of business cards gathered over the years from resources on appointments with Mom—at the court house, the senior center, the mental health office, and the sheriff and police departments. Just in case.

Forty minutes later, Nancy put her suitcase in the back of my car and we headed to Michigan. On the way, she called our prayer chain and shared the situation, then chatted with me about family, pets, and hobbies to help me relax on the four-hour drive.

We found Mom sitting up in bed and able to talk, but with very weak limbs. Mom seemed to think Nancy was her personal nurse and demanded she feed her. Nancy quickly assured me she didn't mind and whispered I might want to go talk with the staff about Mom's prognosis.

The doctor felt Mom would be unlikely to be able to care for herself at home any longer. She said they'd try a few days of medication and rehab, but then Mom might have to go to a nursing home. I recalled dealing with a social worker when a grandchild was in the hospital, so I grabbed my just-in-case pouch of cards and headed for the lobby because that's where the list of staff offices was posted at previous hospitals I'd visited.

I left a message on the social worker's phone and headed for where I thought her office would be located. This hospital seemed to have a similar path to the children's hospital I'd often visited, so I found the correct office within minutes. A startled social worker looked up and asked me where I'd gotten her number and how I found her office, as only the hospital staff knew how to initiate contact. When I explained about our grandson, she was sympathetic and asked how the family handled their loss. I was able to share Dave's story with her. I honestly didn't know at which location I'd found a card with her personal cellphone number, but she suggested I complete paperwork and then spend the next two to three days selecting a nursing home.

In between visits with Mom, Nancy and I toured and observed the area nursing homes. I made an appointment with the administrator for the one I thought best fit Mom's needs. Nancy asked if she could come in, and I couldn't see why not. I had no idea what questions to ask except regarding payment. When the administrator finished answering that one, she turned to Nancy, assuming she was family, and asked if she had any questions. Her quick response of "Actually, yes I do" surprised me. My mouth soon fell open as she began to question ratio of aides to patients, nurses' duties, night staff, physical therapists' hours, the home's Medicare rating, and procedures and equipment. The administrator and I gaped at her, and I could see she felt as I did that my average-appearing friend had some serious knowledge about nursing homes. Other staff members were called in, and those questions were answered to Nancy's satisfaction and my astonishment. Next Nancy asked several situational-response questions, and the administrator complimented me on my appropriately knowledgeable traveling companion.

We left the nursing home with a contract in my hands. As the door closed behind us, I whispered, "Who are you?" Nancy laughed and said she'd worked for twenty years in a nursing home setting. Amazing, isn't it, that God had an expert in my kitchen when the phone rang? Coincidence? I don't think so…and the nursing home and hospital staff agreed.

Life-Changing Lesson: All we need has already been supplied.

It's hard to imagine that when God planned us, He also planned the fulfillment of all our needs. Scripture tells us He's already provided everything pertaining to life and godliness.

Life-Changing Verse:

We'll never comprehend all the great things he does; His miracle-surprises can't be counted (Job 9:10, The Message).

Life-Changing Challenge: Name one miracle-surprise you've experienced.

Write the surprise down then share the event with someone, perhaps the "Nancy" in your life, and thank them for making themselves available for God to bless you through them.

25
Surprise!

In the airport, I was already flying high emotionally from a special encounter with the Native-American clerk in the little airport shop.

Southwest has people line up in groups before boarding. From my assigned spot, I glanced around and was drawn to a young man a few rows over, who was dark-skinned but so much resembled our granddaughter's tall, broad-shouldered and dark-haired boyfriend that at first I thought he was Frank.

Before I could look away, he spotted me staring and smiled. I found myself praying silently and thinking, *I wish I could reach him somehow*, and then scoffed at the thought. All seating is open on Southwest, and he was rows over in the boarding group. What chance was there that a young man would choose to sit by the weird grandma he'd caught staring at him?

I prefer the window seat and asked a fellow in an outside seat if I could slip past him. After settling my purse under the seat, I gazed out the window with camera in hand. I was interrupted from watching the baggage being loaded by a voice asking if he could sit in the middle. I blinked in surprise at the fellow I'd spotted before in the boarding line. While he settled, I prayed with astonishment and asked God to minister through me to meet this young man's needs. Introductions revealed his Native-American name (I'll call him Seneca). We exchanged information about our family history, which included my spiritual journey. Seneca's sincere way of posing questions made me curious about his vocation.

His journey to being a lawyer, including associated success and travel opportunities, was fascinating. I think we were both surprised when I made statements about what he likely had to do before taking a case or making a stand on an issue. God had brought snippets of memories from court appearances with my mother to mind, and Seneca agreed with my observations and explained other things I'd long wondered about. That was a pleasant surprise, but the topic God had planned shocked us both.

Talking about family, Seneca assumed I'd be a matchmaker, and added that no, there was no woman in his life, and he doubted he'd ever get married. I asked why he thought that. He said he'd had a few relationships that didn't work out, and they took way too much work. He concluded that women today were nothing like women of my generation. Then he stressed that he was very happily single, thank you. Processing his reaction, I thought, *Hmm, it seems "thou dost protest too much."* But I was totally shocked at what happened next.

Our eyes had met, and Seneca seemed to be challenging me to see beyond his words. His eyes widened when I met his gaze and asked, "Seneca, why do you think you're too old to know love or to feel loved?" I went on to tell him God wanted him to know he was loved, and God was going to send him a godly woman whom he'd meet in six years.

Yikes! I knew where the "God loves you" part came from, but making a claim that something would happen in a particular time? I slapped my hand over my mouth, expecting him to say I was nutty, but instead his eyes welled up with tears. He leaned toward me and said, "All right. I'll admit my lifelong dream has been to find someone to love me that way."

We were both rather floored with the conversation and the result. I told him I'd never made such a declaration before, but felt I was also to tell him the next years were for him to prepare for this woman so he'd be ready for her because she'd be a godly woman, one he'd meet in church.

"I'm heading home right now," he responded. "My mom will be thrilled to know I'm making a commitment right now to attend church with them and wherever my travels lead— and not just to look for that woman."

I gave him my card so he could contact me when he'd met his dream woman. I'm kind of like Paul Harvey that way. I love to hear the rest of the story.

The flight was soon over, and Seneca was very caring, treating me like his elder by finding my luggage and making sure I was okay and knew where I was going next. The last thing he said when we parted was that he was looking forward to contacting me someday.

And I was thinking, *Wow, God, You are so amazing! I never know what will happen when You want to use me in someone's life. Whether I hear back or not is immaterial. To know I've been chosen to sow seeds of Your Word is enough.*

Life-Changing Lesson: Expect to be surprised.

We're often great at telling God how to solve a problem or respond to a situation, but God wants to surprise us with things more amazing than we can imagine. The next time you ask God to use you in someone's life, expect a surprise.

Life-Changing Verse:

This is my life work: helping people understand and respond to this message. It came as a sheer gift to me, a real surprise, God handling all the details (Ephesians 3:7, The Message).

Life-Changing Challenge:

Let surprise be your new norm. Read all of Ephesians 3 and see how God expects us to share his miracles today through the power of His Spirit. Journal also, so you can watch for His miracles!

26
My Time

Time off? What's that? My mother was safely relocated in a nursing home, and the health worker told me I shouldn't visit her for the first week in order to allow her to acclimate. "Besides," she explained, "there's something you've wanted to do all this time while caring for your mother. Now's your time."

I stared at her. I hadn't told her my dream, and I barely knew her even though she'd been my contact at the agency for six years. Perhaps every family she worked with had dreams of being free from the constant stress of caregiving and guardianship. I continued to wonder about her choice of words.

How could she possibly know that six years ago, just before I'd gotten the call to be guardian, I'd heard of the CLASS (Christian Leaders and Speakers Seminars) conference in New Mexico and had set that as my goal? Even if she did know about that, wouldn't she then also realize there was no way I could afford the conference? I had to put all we had and more into Mom's caregiving.

Still, I went home with the conference on my mind. Might as well look it up on the computer, I thought. Who knows if CLASS is still in existence after all these years? As it turned out, the CLASS conference was still an annual event, and what I saw on the website gave me hope. There was a scholarship!

For the first time in years, I didn't have to be "on call" for a couple of weeks, and thus I felt God saying, *This is the year.* I prayerfully hoped that would be true.

I quickly wrote up the required information and prepared the application. Then I made a huge error with my prayer. I told God He'd obviously be aware that I couldn't afford the conference, so if I didn't get a full scholarship, I couldn't go. I clicked send and rethought my prayer. I'd as much as dared God to get me a complete scholarship! If I was a good parent and my children did that, I'd teach them a lesson—and I knew already that I was in for one. There was no way I was going to win the (one) complete scholarship prize.

And I didn't, but I was awarded a partial scholarship. My tune had changed, and I was now asking God to show me how I could earn or find the rest of the funds needed for registration, housing, and food, plus transportation to New Mexico.

As I prayed, I remembered something an elderly friend gave me fifteen years earlier: a little bag of broken jewelry. Perhaps there might be something there that could be sold for the needed cash. Now where had I put that bag? A few days and a bunch more praying later, I found the bag and had the broken bits of jewelry appraised (and sold)—for the exact balance remaining for the conference cost! Now all I needed was transportation, and $50 each for two critiques.

I shouldn't have been surprised when the phone rang, but I was. A young woman I ministered to over a decade earlier had moved away but was now back in town. She explained that God led her to contact those who'd helped her in her youth and to thank them, so she invited me out to lunch. We had a wonderful visit. After she brought me home and started to drive away, she suddenly turned back. With a finger on her chin, she looked like she wanted to say something.

"What?" I asked, stooping to peer in the open passenger-side window.

Shyly nodding her head, she said I'd probably think she was weird, but she really felt God wanted her to ask me something. With a little encouragement, she explained that she travelled a lot in her new job and got more air miles than she'd ever use. My heart began beating faster with anticipation as she continued. She'd recently received a voucher from an airline and she felt she'd never be able to use the flight by the deadline. Was there a chance I'd like that voucher?

Yes, indeed! The voucher was for one of two airlines that provided transportation from Milwaukee to New Mexico. Perfect!

Humbled, I dared not ask God for that last $50 for a critique. The first $50 had come from an unexpected and unprecedented Election Day bonus the week prior. My daughter joked that every election worker got a bonus because I prayed for a critique.

The day before the trip, I thought I should prepare the material for the second critique just in case something turned up. And it did.

I was one of several people helping an out-of-town friend with household duties after her heart surgery. She was on the phone now, telling me she had to see me that night. Her place of residence was an hour each way from home, but I went immediately, thinking something was wrong and she needed care. I didn't think to ask if she'd contacted any of her family members or even what she needed. I just responded out of instinct, told my husband I'd be gone a few hours, and got in the car.

Moments after my friend and I hugged, she assured me she was fine physically then handed me an envelope and apologized for calling me so late. A sense of urgency, she explained, came to her that she must give me that envelope tonight and then watch me open it. She had no idea what the funds were for, but I knew the moment I saw the envelope that the exact amount for a critique would be within.

This truly was my time—compliments of God and His obedient children.

Life-Changing Lesson: The question often contains the answer.

How often have you, like me, asked God, "Will you?" Instead, knowing His promises, we should be praying, in awe: "You *will*?" Or in anticipation: "You *will*!"

Life-Changing Verse:

Making the most of your time, because the days are evil (Eph. 5:16, NASB).

Life-Changing Challenge:

God once challenged me to spend a day without words, which was one of the most difficult things I've tried. I challenge you, as well, to respond differently next time you're challenged (or in response to your last challenge). See what you can do, how you can respond (instead of react) and communicate through your actions, instead of words.

27

Sweet Surrender

I wasn't being very gracious. "I feel like you're supposed to have this," my friend persisted, pressing the huge maroon, large-print Bible into my hand. "Besides," she joked, "you're not getting any younger, and you never know when you'll need the large print."

I'd thanked her and set the Bible aside, forgetting about it until one day at work I got an inter-office phone call.

Only a few weeks had passed since my teacher-friend Patti had experienced sudden but alarming lapses in memory. Forgetting to post something on the board was unnerving, but the clincher came the night she couldn't remember which exit to take to drop off the friend and neighbor with whom she'd been carpooling for years. She'd joked how the repeated route became automatic, and Patti's confusion prompted her neighbor to urge her to call a doctor. The next morning Patti left her friend at work and went to her appointment. We who knew her collectively held our breath when the call came only hours later. That call brought a diagnosis of malignant brain tumors.

Surgery quickly followed. When Patti called the Business Education department with an update of her condition, she sent a message to tell me her vision was now impaired and she hoped I'd know where to get her a large-print Bible.

A silent wonder filled me as I thought about the maroon gift my friend Irene had so teasingly offered me. I passed the Bible to Patti's neighbor at school the next day, and knew the gift would be delivered that evening.

Two days later a pink message slip told me to call Patti. I was awed to hear her say, "I think you have what I need. Would you come see me?"

Honored, yet fearful, I prayed frantically during the forty-five-minute drive to her home. I had haunting memories of walking up to the funeral home after my father died, thinking, *So this is grief.* My mind filled with doubt. How could I help someone through a valley I'd never been through and didn't even like to think about? She said I had something she wanted. Not *some* thing, the Spirit whispered. *Some*one*!*

I bowed my head in quick surrender, walked up to her door, and knocked. As the door swung open, I was shocked that I scarcely recognized Patti. Her face and bald head were swollen from medication, and the only hair the brain surgery and chemo had left was a limp rooster-comb patch that drooped above her forehead.

Aching for the loss of the tall, willowy, hula-hoop-crazy high school teacher, I silently mourned every missing strand of her signature chin-length blonde tresses. Looking into her familiar blue eyes, I found the friend and co-worker who'd called the day before saying, "I think you have what I need."

Now those eyes gleamed in eagerness, and her familiar voice echoed from within the distorted body that even she quietly admitted was no longer recognizable as her own.

"Save visiting for later," she said. As clearly as if she'd written them across her classroom chalkboard, those few words emphasized to me that she knew she was dying and had no time to waste.

While praying throughout the forty-five-minute drive to her home, three portions of Scripture had come to mind, but now I stood mute and stunned before her grace. The sight of her struggling to hand me the huge maroon Bible snapped me to attention. I pulled a TV table next to the sofa and set the Bible on top. Patti smiled, touched the book reverently, and simply said, "Show me."

I pointed out John 5:24, and she slowly read the verse, her fingers lightly tracing each word. *With love*, I remember thinking. When she came to the words "no condemnation," she let out a gasp of delight and clasped her left hand to her heart.

In my trance of empathy, I was about to go on to the next verse when she grabbed my wrist in a desperate grasp with the other hand and cried, "Wait! Get a highlighter." Surprised, I went to the table she indicated and returned with the yellow marker. The tumor, she explained, was affecting short-term memory, and though she might forget who visited or if she'd had lunch, she didn't want to forget God's words. Once the bright yellow outlined the words for later reference, she sighed, momentarily contented.

"Okay," she said, like an eager child. "I'm ready now for the next one." Her voice rose in excitement as she read 1 John 5:11-13, especially the portion that stated "…these things were written that you can know that you have eternal life." When she read the word "know," she held the edge of her cushion as if she were about to leap up and dance. "I can know, I can know," she chanted. "I don't have to wonder or hope anymore. I can *know*."

Reverently, I watched as she marked the verse. Then she surprised me by reading the verse again, this time putting her name in place of the word "you," now reading in wonder, "I, Patti, can *know*." Her happy laughter was contagious, and I sat back and joined her, watching her face glow with joy.

Finally we looked into the first chapter of Ephesians and talked about all we have and are in Christ. Six yellow-highlighted words (chosen, predestined, redemption, forgiveness, inheritance, and hope) became wet with our mingling tears as we hugged and prayed. Then we talked about goals she wanted to reach before she died and ways they could be accomplished.

Her assurance settled, she shared a verse of the song "If You Could See Me Now" as one she prayed her family and friends would experience, and other songs she liked to use as prayers. We sang and prayed with abandon until her family arrived, and I prepared to leave.

Humbled and awed as I drove home, I replayed Patti's sweet surrender to the Lord and her excitement and reactions to verses and concepts I'd known for years…and perhaps had begun to take for granted. Although she asked me to come to give her comfort, I realized that in the face of her overflowing joy, I'd also been given a gift, for I knew I'd lost the fear of death. Fear was gone, and with certainty I could even tell why—there simply was no room for fear. The negative emotion had been replaced, pushed out, and overcome by the reality of the power of God's Word. I'd been caught in the tsunami of Patti's joy and assurance, as God's presence washed over her and spilled onto me. For once I didn't care that I couldn't carry a tune, and I wove my way home singing through my tears: "The wonder of it all, the wonder of it all, just to think that God loves me."[2]

I still pray for Patti's family and friends, that they will also come to see and know the face of God. In remembrance, I wear a little gold pin that spells out "Hope."

Go ahead. Ask me what my pin means. I'd love to share how Patti found hope through sweet surrender and a large-print Bible.

Life-Changing Lesson: Live like someone is watching.

I had no idea Patti was observing my faith-walk at work. Who knows who else is watching us as we go about our daily business of life? What a difference we can make!

I once danced with abandon, totally unselfconscious and without thought of what someone might think. Like the Bible's story of Hannah praying with abandon was misinterpreted by the priest who thought she was drunk, we want to be careful of how we act when we think no one is watching. Patti reminded me that someone is always watching. We can retain that free abandon as long as we remember *someone* is always watching.

Life-Changing Verse:

Now that I've put you there on a hilltop, on a light stand—shine! Keep open house; be generous with your lives. By opening up to others, you'll prompt people to open up with God, this generous Father in heaven (Matthew 5:16, The Message).

Life-Changing Challenge:

To shine, in this verse, according to Strong's Concordance, is "to make visible or known—or be made visible or known." Whether we try or not, we'll be known for our actions, and the truth of our heart condition will be visible through those actions. Would the actions have been different if we'd remembered that someone was watching? Let us live with no regrets…and be a visible child of God.

145

Outline your activities yesterday or another recent day. Next to each activity, list what conclusions others could come to from what they saw (or heard). Ask God to help you live like someone is watching. We know He is…and others are too!

∞28∞
Recalculate!

When the Honey-Bunnies (Daddy's nickname for his girls) get together, things happen.

Our first sister-trip was to Disney World. We dressed alike, and people kept asking, "Are you somebody?" Happy to be "recognized," we posed for dozens of pictures. Years went by before we got together again, aghast at our first restaurant stop to realize we all qualified for the senior discount.

My sister Marlene and I attempted to plan the trip to help our younger sister, Marvel, empty the storage unit she'd paid into and complained about for years. Each time we'd e-mail plans, Marvel would try to postpone with "As soon as…" she started or finished something. Marlene, the organizer, had had enough. Long-distance calls from her are rare, so when caller ID revealed her number, I answered with concern.

"What's wrong?"

"Nothing. I just figured Marvel's delays will go on forever if we don't do something."

"Like?"

"Like, I'll be packed in an hour, and I'll see you in the morning."

"Tomorrow?"

"Yes!" She laughed. "Try to get some sleep; we have a lot of driving to do."

We meshed plans: mine to see Nashville, Amelia Island, and three friends who lived along our path; Marlene's to see Dollywood, friends in North Carolina, and a son in Florida we'd visit on the way home.

Marvel's response, after the shock settled, was unexpected. She wanted to ride back with us, visit her daughter, a friend in Tennessee, and Elvis' Graceland, and then fly home from Wisconsin. An hour later, Marlene and I began our drive to Ohio for the night. In the morning, we gathered an armful of tourist brochures and decided to see or at least drive by as many attractions as we could. Our devotional was from Psalm 91, and the part telling us God ordered his angels "to guard you wherever you go" had us chuckling. So many things happen to me that family and friends joke I need a legion of angels guarding me rather than the usual single guardian angel. My sister teased that "angels" was plural, and so we were covered.

We headed south, laughing and zipping in and out of flea-markets, caves, and gem mines. Instead of two days, we took a week to get to Florida. But we did get there, and only because something happened.

Just outside of Nashville, the GPS went wacky; the dial indicating direction was spinning like two magnets facing off. The voice in the box repeatedly directed continuous turns around a deserted gas station.

I finally pulled onto the cracked blacktop of the vacant parking lot, and we yanked out maps. We checked our printed route to decide what to do. I wanted to show Marlene the Opryland Hotel and have supper nearby before moving on.

Deep in discussion and grousing about the GPS, we were startled when a southern drawl called, "Y'all need help?"

We looked at each other. Neither of us had seen a car at the station during our dizzying circular route, nor had we heard one pull up, but the chuckle of the sandy-haired guy in overalls indicated he'd watched my red Vibe do the loop-de-loop. His "round and round and round she goes" comment confirmed he'd been watching, and we burst out laughing. We told him about our Nashville plans and the GPS, asking for directions for the next turnoff into town.

"Where you heading next?" he asked.

Odd question. "Asheville," we answered.

"Well, you can always see Nashville on the way back," he suggested. "That Cumberland Gap drive is real pretty. 'Sides, you won't have much time before dark to spend in Nashville. You want to be able to see your way around a strange town."

His uncommon concern was touching. Dusk was falling, and we thought, *Why not?* We'd see Nashville on the way back as he'd suggested. He brushed off our thanks and pointed us to Cumberland Gap Highway and Asheville.

The moment the car glided onto the Cumberland ramp, the GPS made a *zzzzzzip* sound, and the maps came back on—suddenly working fine. Huh!

Marlene drove, and I photographed beautiful scenery until huge black clouds rolled toward us and blew overhead. Marlene commented that someone behind us was going to get quite the storm.

The big-screen TV in the hotel's breakfast room the next morning shockingly reviewed the flooding we'd escaped in Nashville. We prayed for those affected and wondered again at the GPS insanity and the mysterious man's directions.

Blocks shy of our Asheville lunch destination, we stopped to check out street vendors on foot. We were just steps away from entering our selected eatery when sirens blared and police blocked off the street due to a fire — in that very restaurant! We explained to the nearby vendor how we'd just missed the flooding in Nashville, and now this. We jokingly asked for a "safe" restaurant recommendation. Laughing, he suggested an international experience, Jerusalem Garden Café, remarking as we turned away that he'd better head inside to call and warn them we were on the way.

Perhaps he was right. There *was* a breakfast incident after a carriage ride in Savannah, and other adventures such as using Marlene's arm for a windshield-wiper the last hour to Lake Worth, almost getting heat stroke at the storage unit, getting lost on the way home, the three-breasted chicken at Sawgrass, and being proposed to by the Carter brothers.

By the time we'd completed our 5,000-mile round-trip, those angels must have been exhausted.

Life-Changing Lesson: I have protectors watching over me.

Knowing God does send angels to protect us doesn't mean we should take unnecessary risks, but it does mean we can be thankful for dangers that have been averted.

Life-Changing Verse:

Do not neglect to show hospitality to strangers, for by this some have entertained angels without knowing it (Hebrews 13:2, NASB).

Life-Changing Challenge: Discern God's Spirit in others.

Have you ever met a stranger with whom you instantly felt a spiritual connection? I've had that happen to me many times, and I nearly always learn they're brothers or sisters in the Lord.

Show hospitality to one of these brethren this month, preferably someone you don't know very well, and then try to make these meetings a habit every month. A dear elderly saint used to refer to this type of intentional hospitality as "angel practice."

~29~
Go Wednesday

Go Wednesday! Go Wednesday! I'd been visiting my Mom on Mondays for almost two years. I'd particularly chosen Monday because the nursing home had a non-denominational devotional and singing time that day, and Mom loved it. She also had a favorite cousin who was sometimes available to join us for lunch on Mondays. The nursing home staff had confirmed nothing special was occurring on Wednesday, but still the inner voice kept on. My friend Marge usually came with me, and I called her to see what she thought.

When I explained that all week a subliminal urging to go on Wednesday had me wondering why, her response was a gracious form of "Duh!" She let me know she believed God was trying to get through to me, so why not go Wednesday and see what happens?

Unless there were special appointments or concerns, we tried to make the trip in one day: four hours there, visit, have lunch with Mom, visit more, and head home. That was our plan for this trip as well. As usual I prayed about what I should bring and spotted a book I'd just reviewed,

Simple Faith by Eddie Snipes. The book was an excellent Bible-driven primer for new believers about doctrine. Part of reviewing for me is praying—for the message and purpose of the book to be accomplished, and for the person who'll receive and read the book to understand the message. I'd just ordered a half-dozen for the church office, so why not take this one along? I tossed *Simple Faith* into my Michigan bag with other supplies I might need.

The trip up was uneventful, and Mom actually slept a majority of the time we were there. She groggily begged the aides to dress her and help her sit up, but she promptly fell asleep after all that effort. In her waking moments, we talked and prayed briefly then left at our usual time.

"Well," I said to Marge on the drive home, "I'm not sure what 'go Wednesday' was about."

When we saw the mileage sign to a little town halfway home, Marge asked if we were going to stop there to see Nancy. Six years prior, when I first started caring for my mom, I'd passed a new little store off the highway and stopped in to see what was there. I'd met Nancy, and we became friends—bonded, oddly enough, by cancer. Her husband and my grandson had the same type, so we compared notes and promised to pray for one another. I assumed she was a believer because she referred to prayer. I gave her Randy Alcorn's book *Heaven,* which had helped my grandson. She read the book to her husband and said he found the words greatly comforting and led him to the assurance he was reading about his destination.

Every trip didn't end at Nancy's shop, depending on my mom's appointments, how late we left, and if we got that far before the shop closed. Even though visits were irregular, we'd grown close, and I looked forward to stopping and catching up on one another's lives.

This night we pulled into the lot and saw a new sign on the door. "Hours changed—closed Mondays and Tuesdays." Marge and I exchanged glances. "Good thing we didn't come on Monday," she said, shrugging her shoulders.

I opened the door to the shop and got a huge surprise. Nancy rushed toward me from across the shop, her arms open wide. "You came! You came!" she cried.

Wrapped in her arms, I rejoiced in her happiness and wondered aloud, "You were expecting me? But I usually come on Monday."

"I know," she said. "But I prayed and told God I really wish Delores could come today. I have so many questions, and I just knew you'd have a book to give me." A book? The one in the car? Wow. What was this about?

Nancy eagerly explained what had happened. Since her husband and my grandson both passed away, she'd been reading our David's testimony every night for a month. "Last night, I got it!"

I frowned. "Got what, Nancy?"

I felt my eyes grow wider and saw Marge's were doing the same as Nancy explained she'd always considered herself "religious" and hadn't really understood her husband's deepening faith as he read the material on heaven. She struggled to understand the Bible he'd encouraged her to read. This past week, reading David's testimony again and asking God to help her understand, she said she "got it." She'd grabbed her Bible and began reading as if it were a new book. She couldn't get enough of it.

After jumping up and down and rejoicing awhile, I asked Nancy about her comment that I'd probably bring her a book. She explained she was having difficulty understanding some of the "big concepts" in the Bible, listing several basic doctrines as examples. She figured I'd help her find a book that could help her understand what she was reading. Explanations of those doctrines was an exact description of the book I'd felt led to bring along.

Her new and simple faith surprised us both when I told her I had the perfect book in the car, and she simply smiled and said, "I figured that would happen."

She closed up the shop, and we had a wonderful time answering her questions, explaining Scripture, and encouraging her. A double round of hugs, and we had to leave. Marge and I were heading out the driveway, sharing snippets back and forth that all began with, "Wasn't it amazing…?"

I hit the brakes and looked at Marge. Together we said, "Go Wednesday!"

Life-Changing Lesson: When in doubt, get good counsel.

There have been too many times I ignored the prompting of the Spirit or doubted the outcome of His direction. When we feel a repeated urging to do something, we need to investigate. Three equally important aspects of that investigation are praying about it, seeing if the prompting agrees with God's Word, and seeking good counsel (someone who will tell us the truth based upon God's Word and not just tell what they think you want to hear).

Life-Changing Verse:

Form your purpose by asking for counsel, then carry it out using all the help you can get (Proverbs 20:18, The Message).

Life-Changing Challenge:

Prepare for the next time you have any doubt about a plan, a purpose, or a challenge. Create a list of resources for godly counsel you can trust. Agree to be available to one another and to pray together to seek God's wisdom. Accept help in carrying out the objective. The body of Christ working together is part of God's purpose for His Church.

30

Impossible Dream

Whenever I hear opportunity knocking, I try to be the first to get to the door.

So when my friend Marla said her sister LeAnn was headed to Spain to teach English, I took about a minute to dial her number. Within hours, a confirmation e-mail welcomed me to a team committed to the two-week teaching experience.

Nineteen years prior, I visited Spain on a trip with high-school students and staff. I almost wasn't accepted for an adult-student-family stay because the Spanish travel director thought such a stay was impossible. When he shared my information with a pastor, he was told of Juana and Raphael Gomez, a couple who requested an older student. They accepted my profile, and the impossible became reality. Teacher-friends teased that Raphael's *cuchilleria* (cutlery) hobby meant *me* on the revolving wheel of a knife-thrower! They also thought my memorizing Steve Green's Spanish songs, hoping they'd be useful, was silly. We were mutually amazed when I met the family, and their car radio was blaring those same songs. I was also relieved to discover Raphael actually made knives and scissors with a foot-pedaled grindstone and hand-bellows.

Memorable trips to a convent, the market, a traditional and a contemporary church service, picnicking at the camp home they'd just bought to remodel, and going to a park with scissors and a plastic bag to find fresh herbs all brought us closer together. When the time came to leave, our tearful good-byes were "until heaven." Anything else seemed truly impossible—until now.

Impossible was imagining the Gomez's daughter Nohemi would find me on Facebook and ask if I was the Delores who stayed with them. She'd seen my excited post: "I'm going to Spain! I'm going to Spain!" She hinted she lived only 400 miles from the English camp location.

I longed to relive singing and worshipping in Spanish and picnicking at their camp, but how? Imagine the thrill when someone saw our Facebook conversation and sent a gift specifically for expenses after the mission trip. Suddenly the impossible dream was a possibility. I felt amazingly loved and over-the-top excited—until my husband nixed the plan unless I had a bilingual companion.

English Camp leaders had offered to bring me to the fast-train after camp, but Ken was uncomfortable with me traveling alone overseas, especially with my limited Spanish. Ken suggested we pray for a traveling companion who spoke Spanish. *Honestly*, I thought, *who's going to just happen to be in or near Osuna, speak Spanish, be either working at or near the English camp, and be willing to escort me to my Spain family?* As impossible and unrealistic as the request seemed, we prayed together that night and were totally blown away by a phone call the next morning.

A good friend who's proficiently bilingual cheerfully greeted me when I answered. "I've been thinking about taking a mission trip somewhere this summer," she said. "I wondered if you were going anywhere." Excitedly I explained about the English camp in Spain and the desire to visit my host family after camp. "Count me in!" she declared, adding that another friend might also be interested—and she was.

That's where I pinched myself to see if I was awake.

The time at English camp flew by. Classes and homework were designed and executed daily. The work was exhausting but rewarding. I was living an impossible dream.

The morning after the school graduation, we were on the Avé, Spain's fast-train, getting us to Nohemi's in under two hours with an amazingly smooth ride. The only thing I regretted was arriving on a Sunday, thinking I'd miss that special memory of Spanish praise and worship.

The Gomez hugs were non-stop, and so were the dream-come-true moments. Juana quickly whisked us into a *tapas* bar for breakfast then led us down the block to a little church. Amazingly, the English camp training theme, "Don't try to be a lone ranger," was reflected in the message. When I heard *Cuan Grande Es El* (How Great Thou Art), happy tears overflowed. The impossible had come true.

We walked everywhere in Ciudad Real (the royal city), visiting parks, shops, museums, Don Quixote tableaus, and Puerta de Toledo, the only remaining part of the 14th-century city walls. We had ice cream in the central plaza, still glowing with sunlight at 9:30 p.m.

The old world and the new conjoined at the Gomez's home. The bakery truck still came by daily, contrasting with an updated kitchen and electricity in Raphael's shop. He still fashioned cutlery and iron Quixotes there, but the sharpening millstone and hand-billows were now repurposed as patio decorations.

Stone walls now surrounded the white-plastered camp-home I

remembered, and a life-sized Don Quixote overlooked the garden. Raphael picked vegetables for *gazpacho* soup while we plucked grapes from the arbor. And of course, we explored the wooded property. A rustic iron merry-go-round with a different metal animal caricature at each seat, a castle-like playhouse, and an Alice-in-Wonderland mushroom-shaped stone table and rock chairs, evidenced grandchildren. Palm fronds formed a roofed shelter, and blue tiles outlined the ancient baker's oven, a spring well, and a flourmill, all original to the 600-year-old house. Nearby, plastic work buckets and electrical cords seemed out of place, giving a feel of having one foot in each century.

In the waning sunset, we climbed outside stairs to the top of the house for stargazing. I turned on my phone app, and Raphael thrilled at the music and identified various constellations as we rotated on a little platform, my phone raised to the sky. Later Juana gave me the greatest compliment, telling me I was like a spiritual vitamin. She said I was an answer to their prayer for a way they could help the youth of their community. When they heard about the English camp, they felt their impossible dream had also become a possibility.

Back in the States, unpacking my metal Don Quixote, I smiled, finally understanding some of the story. A quixotic personality like mine—an impulsive and unpredictable dream chaser—can actually be a benefit, particularly for seeing the rest of a story and fighting the right giants. Accompanied by trusty companions who also believe in the God who does the impossible, life couldn't get any better.

Life-Changing Lesson: God wants to bless me.

Part of the baggage of my past was to listen to the words of Satan that God would only want me as a conduit to others. God, however, calls me Beloved, His child, and clearly shows me that *He is more interested in developing my character than in developing my ministry.*

Life-Changing Verse:

Delight yourself in the LORD; And He will give you the desires of your heart (Psalm 37:4, NASB).

Life-Changing Challenge: Ask myself daily: is God my precious choice?

Ask myself daily: is God my precious-choice (exquisite, chosen, most quality) relationship, my most precious friend, my desire, my delight? An epitaph that implied to know this departed person was to love him inspired a love song years ago that spoke of how the more you get to know about a good person the more you would love him. The thought also expresses our relationship with God, because the more we study His character and come to know Him, the more we are drawn to love Him. The names of God do that for me. They explain His character, drawing me to know Him and to love Him. A fun challenge: see if you can name a characteristic of God that begins with each letter of the alphabet.

~31~
A.G.W.C.

Laughing out loud, I continued walking the neighborhood, not caring if the neighbors hadn't already figured out I talk to God when I walk—or that He often talks back and says the funniest things.

My grandkids were excitedly preparing for their first week away at Camp Awana. I was praying for them and thinking I should send them mail, when God interrupted that thought with one of His own: *What about the kids who don't get any mail?*

"What about them?" I wondered aloud.

Won't they feel sad? Won't they wish they had a grandma who wrote to them? What if you wrote a letter like you were their *grandma?*

What a fun picture, to imagine a little girl or boy who got no mail all week, suddenly getting something at mail call. *Yes, God, I'll do it. That's such a great idea! I'd never have thought of it myself.*

I know.

And that's when I burst out laughing.

And mission A.G.W.C. began. I wrote the letter sitting on the back porch swing, imagining what I'd say to a suddenly adopted and very much loved extra grandchild. The signature gave me pause. I didn't want to write my name, but I didn't want to leave the note unsigned. A heart prayer went up for direction.

He answered immediately. *Who are you going to be to them?*

Oh, just a grandma who cares, I thought.

A.G.W.C. (A Grandma Who Cares) quickly became my Camp Awana signature and pen name.

The letter was fun to write as I pictured the preteens at my grandkids' camp. That awkward age where your body, mind, and emotions are all over the place, and you wish you had someone who understood and would really listen—and not talk back. Prayers followed letters addressed to "A girl who got no mail yet this week" and "A boy who got no mail yet this week." They were mailed after camp started so they'd arrive near the end of the week. Camp directors thought my letters a fun idea and later told me about the surprising number of excited hands waving to get those letters. But more surprising were the responses.

I thought I'd been cute to only put AGWC in the upper left corner of the envelope, but the mailman requested I add my address. Some of the kids took advantage of that and wrote back.

Some were sweet thank-you notes for helping them feel "not so lonesome." Others wrote that they never knew their grandma and thought getting a letter from one was fun. I even got a couple of notes from parents, one appreciative for giving them the idea to write letters to their own children when they were away at camp, and one asking if I'd be their child's pen-pal until next year's camp.

The children sent prayer requests about all the situations we read about that are only statistics until a name or face is attached to them. Things like "My parents are divorced, and I have one set until Wednesday at noon, and then another set for the rest of the week. Sometimes I wake up and can't remember whose house I'm at." Or "How come some kids are so mean?" or "Why don't I have friends?" That last query was from a girl who wrote a several-page missive of defense about her good qualities and why others should want her as a friend. Along with my response, I copied her letter (with all the I's highlighted) and chatted about the difference between John 3:30 and lots of attention to self. When I explained how Jesus gave her all those abilities so she could let His love shine through her to many people—some who wish they had her abilities—she got the message. She began focusing on being a friend rather than being miffed that others didn't respond to her continually marketing herself.

This girl and others who asked if I'd write them back got two letters, one to them and one to their parents, asking for permission to be a pen-pal until next year's camp. A select few chose to write for several years and later adopted the practice to be a mystery friend pen-pal.

God's novel idea expanded to kids at our church camp and inspired me to write starter notes to troubled teens. "Care to talk about it?" or "I'll listen" often opened up a floodgate of needs and led to some of the most rewarding experiences of my life.

God knew, no matter where I went, there'd be people who needed a grandma who cares. Wow. Listening when you pray sure pays!

Life-Changing Lesson: I heard God speak when I was listening.

Sometimes our prayer is only talking. Pausing while reading God's Word, inclining my heart and quieting my mind to listen for His teaching and instruction, is when I "hear" His voice. God expects me to give a similar respect to those with whom I share His words. Do I really hear others speak, or am I thinking how I'll respond? If I give the words of others respect, they're more likely to take heed of mine.

Life-Changing Verse:

Then Moses said, "What if they will not believe me or listen to what

I say? For they may say, 'The LORD has not appeared to you'" (Exodus 4:1, NASB).

Life-Changing Challenge:

Moses' concerns were legitimate possibilities of the risk, but they also exhibited a lack of trust in God and a desire to know or have control of the outcome of the situation beforehand. My calling (or ability) isn't to make others believe what I've heard; my calling is to obey and do as the Lord leads. Moses' fears came to pass many times, and he took a while to learn he wasn't responsible for others' reactions. God gives everyone a choice, and He also gives everyone a longing to be heard. Your challenge is to learn from Moses. Write an "I'm listening" note as God directs then send the letter off with a prayer. If you journal, add the name and date and the word "listening" to today's entry. Leave a space to record the rest of the story.

∾32∽
Last Things First

This is how I plan my days: I start dinner before breakfast. Only then can I write a list for the day because I make certain that if nothing else goes right or gets done, the most important thing I want done at day's end will be completed. In other words, I do the last thing first.

If meals and bills, writing goals, relationships, and family time (all temporal things) are that important, doesn't making certain that eternal things are also taken care of first make sense?

Knowing that God in His mercy considered us each worth dying for, wouldn't such love beg investigation? Knowing He further promised to provide everything we need pertaining to life and godliness, shouldn't we be eager to first make time to search how we can be equipped to share His amazing grace?

What's stopping us from doing last things first?

Barriers to Hearing God's Voice

God is always pleased to reveal His will to us. But at times, we can't receive the message. Something in our life is creating a barrier to hearing Him. *Self-will* is one of those obstacles. Sometimes, we decide what we're going to do without God's input. We still talk to Him about our plan, even thinking it's so logical the Lord must agree. But we've stopped listening for His will.

Influence is another obstacle. It's wise to seek godly counsel, but believers must be careful whom they allow to influence them. Many people will say what someone else wants to hear rather than what's actually needed.

Sin is a third barrier. It hinders our ability to know God's will. First, our spirit is clouded so we can't determine His mind. Second, the Father may not reveal the next step in His plan because He's waiting for us to repent and become willing to obey.

Distraction is yet another obstacle for believers. One of the most subtle obstructions to knowing God's will is busyness. Our hands and minds are so full we don't have the patience to wait and listen. The Lord doesn't chase after us, trying to force us to hear Him. Psalm 46:10 says, "Be still, and know that I am God." That's God's simple solution for clearing the clutter of overbooked lives.

The next time you seem unable to determine the Lord's will, try slowing down so you can focus on Him. Then consider whether you might have allowed one of these barriers to be constructed between you and God. Ask, and He will gladly help you to dismantle it.[3]

Psalm 119: 9-16 (The Message)

How can a young person live a clean life?
By carefully reading the map of your Word.
I'm single-minded in pursuit of you;
Don't let me miss the road signs you've posted.
I've banked your promises in the vault of my heart
so I won't sin myself bankrupt.
Be blessed, God; train me in your ways of wise living.

I'll transfer to my lips all the counsel that comes from your mouth;
I delight far more in what you tell me about living
than in gathering a pile of riches.
I ponder every morsel of wisdom from you,
I attentively watch how you've done it.
I relish everything you've told me of life,
I won't forget a word of it.

The Most Important Miracle

Imagine that! Almighty God longs to have us experience the greatest miracle of all—eternal hope and peace and satisfaction that nothing in the world can bring. A relationship with the living God is available because He's provided the means to make it happen. Life's most important question is this: Will you go to heaven when you die?

Notice it isn't a question of how good you are. As a matter of fact, understanding that we're sinners helps us realize that only Jesus was pure enough to pay the penalty for our sin. Imagine getting called before a judge for a lifetime of tickets and crime then finding out someone had stepped in and taken your penalty! Romans 5:8 (NASB) says, "But God demonstrates His own love to us, in that while we were still sinners, Christ died for us."

If you understand you're a sinner, and if you believe Jesus Christ came as the one and only Redeemer of sin, there's only one question remaining: are you ready to implement God's plan by receiving the gift of His Son, Jesus Christ, as your Redeemer, Messiah, and Lord? That would be the most important miracle you could ever witness or experience.

If you made this decision, or want more information, please contact me at: deloresliesner.com or e-mail – delores7faith@yahoo.com. I'll be excited to welcome you into the family! Here are some resources with a fuller explanation of how to have a personal relationship with God:

www.**cru.org/how-to-know-god**

Our Daily Bread - http://odb.org/

http://knowhim.afr.net

http://billygraham.org/grow-your-faith/

The Navigators – How to study a Bible Verse:

http://www.navigators.org/Tools/Newsletters/Featured%20 Newsletters/One%20To%20One/April%202011/April%20 2011/Building%20Blocks%20for%20Understanding%20a%20 Bible%20Verse

Endnotes

1. – Song Title "Be Not Afraid"

1 Text: Based on Isaiah 43:2–3; Luke 6:20ff. © 1975, 1978, Robert J. Dufford, SJ and OCP. All rights reserved. Used by permission.

2 "The Wonder of It All," words and music by George Beverly Shea. 1956 (Renewed) Word Music, LLC. All rights reserved. Used by permission.

3 Barriers to Hearing God's Voice, published by AllAboutGod.com Ministries, M. Houdmann, P. Matthews-Rose, R. Niles, editors, 2002-2014. Used by permission.